A VIKING
WAY OF LIFE

A VIKING WAY OF LIFE

Combs and Communities in Early Medieval Britain

STEVEN P. ASHBY

AMBERLEY

First published 2014

Amberley Publishing
The Hill, Stroud
Gloucestershire, GL5 4EP

www.amberley-books.com

British Library Cataloguing in Publication Data.
A catalogue record for this book is available from the British Library.

ISBN 978 1 4456 0152 6 (paperback)
ISBN 978 1 4456 2058 9 (ebook)

Typeset in 10pt on 12pt Sabon.
Typesetting and Origination by Amberley Publishing.
Printed in the UK.

CONTENTS

Acknowledgements

No piece of research, however framed, is ever truly independent, and this book owes an immense debt to a large number of people. First, thanks are due to Dr James Barrett, who first kindled and supervised my interest in Viking-Age combs and combmaking. Professors Terry O'Connor and Julian Richards – once mentors, now also colleagues – deserve an enormous amount of credit. The world of combs is small, but within this community, I have benefited from discussion with a number of researchers including – but certainly not limited to – Arthur MacGregor, Ian Riddler, Gitte Hansen, Andrea Smith, Colleen Batey, Martin Foreman, Andy Heald and Nicky Rogers. Thanks also to the numerous curators who have granted access to their collections; these include Kent Andersson (Statens Historiska Museet, Stockholm); Axel Christophersen (NTNU, Trondheim); Sten Tesch (Sigtuna); Bjorn Ambrosiani (Birka Project); Richard Hall and Christine McDonnell (York Archaeological Trust); Andrew Morrison (York Museums Trust); Thomas Cadbury (Lincoln Museums and Galleries); Rose Nicholson (North Lincs Museum); Anne Brundle and Lynda Aiano (Orkney Museum); David Clarke, Andy Heald and Martin Goldberg (Museum of Scotland); Tommy Watt (Shetland Museum); Gitte Hansen (Bergen Museum). I am grateful to Hayley Saul, Pat Walsh, Alyssa Scott, Nick Griffiths and Sven Schoeder for their illustrations, and to all who allowed me to use their photographs or reproduce their original drawings (particular thanks to Alison Leonard and Ross Docherty for their photography and canoe-steering skills). I am very grateful to the community of staff and students at the University of York, in particular Rob Collins, Emma Waterton, Leslie Johansen and Hayley Saul, all of whom have had to listen to my droning on about combs at one point or another; to Ben Elliot for discussion on the deer–human relationship; and to Tania Dickinson and Mark Edmonds, who have variously encouraged me to develop different aspects of my work. Most of all, I should thank my family, and in particular my wife Aleks, who has had to bear the brunt of this, and Bill, the new arrival, whose keyboard-punching contributions have, unfortunately, had to be edited out. I should also thank Alex Bennett at Amberley for his editorial expertise and patience. Anything good about this book has emerged through discussion with the above named people. The rest is my fault.

It is a terrible shame that Anne Brundle never lived to see this book; I can only hope that she approves, and apologise that I didn't title it *Comby Nations*. This is for you, Anne.

The truth behind Orkney's reindeer combs. (Cartoon by Anne Brundle)

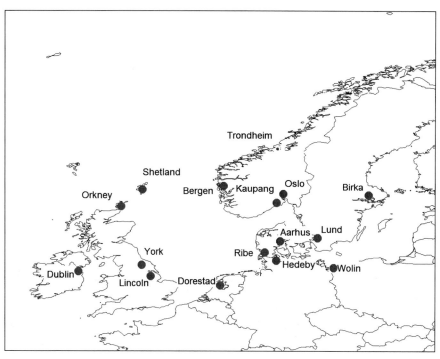

Localities mentioned in the text and other key sites of the Viking Age. (Drawn by
Steve Ashby)

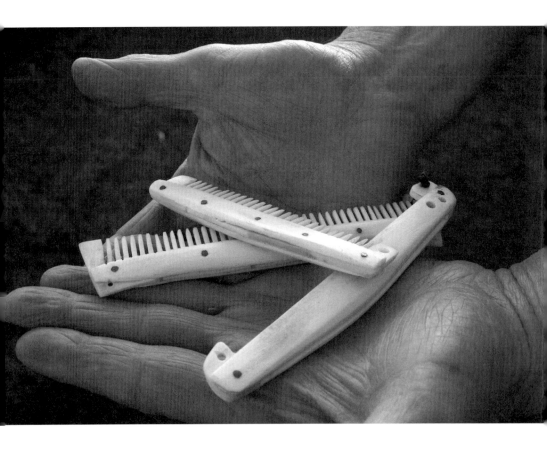

1

Introduction

It's market day, winter, AD 1000. A man is walking down Coppergate, a busy street in the northern town of Jorvik. He pushes through a crowd of people huddled together beside a small booth; someone inside is selling something, who knows what. He sidesteps children playing knucklebones in the street, as well as a dog that, fixated upon a stolen bone, is oblivious to his presence. He smells roasting meat, dried fish, rotting fruit. He hears the sound of traders hawking wooden cups and plates, woollen clothes, and jewellery: some pieces in amber, speaking of eastern shores, others of gilded metal, and of dubious provenance. He notes familiar faces and foreign costumes, local accents and alien dialects, the sounds of raucous laughter and bitter dispute. And then he reaches the stall he's been looking for.

The building consists of a small, low-standing wooden structure, with a thatched roof supported by rather insubstantial oak uprights, and overlying a timber-lined cellar. Just visible in the walls, cracks between timbers are packed with moss, and inside the building the walls are patchily lined with skins and rough textiles, while the floor is damp, uneven and strewn in places with debris of all kinds. From behind the building – where a small animal pen and a number of foul-smelling pits are visible – it is just possible to hear the sounds of chopping and sawing. Spread out on the ground in front of the property is a wickerwork mat, and on this lie all manner of objects: pins, needles, ice skates, fittings for belts and swords, and strange objects that must be something to do with textile manufacture, all with the subtle lustre of freshly worked bone. Most striking of all are a familiar collection of objects notable at first for the lack of polish that gives them away as being made of deer antler, rather than bone. For all their duller finish, their appearance is nonetheless arresting. There are a range of forms, some long, some short, some that perfectly preserve the graceful curve of the antler from which they were cut, others much shorter and more regular, as if closely following a well-understood template. Some have handles, others do not, and there is a wide range of ornament, from the familiar 'ring and dot' design that has been common to personal objects for generations past, to the carefully spaced arrangements of chevrons that must represent a new fashion, perhaps from overseas. Each object consists of many small, strangely shaped pieces of antler, carefully riveted together to form a recognisable whole. Most impressive of all are the arrays of teeth along the long axes of the objects: perfectly straight, even, tapered to a gentle point, and so fine that five teeth occupy a space only about the width of a fingertip.

These objects are, of course, hair combs, and they are the chief reason for our protagonist's venturing out to market today. After he has spent a few moments inspecting the objects, and identified a comb that seems appropriate, the noise from the rear of the workshop ceases, and the artisan comes forward to greet his customer. This combmaker seems familiar. Was he here last year? Certainly it will be worth remembering him, as he can make a good comb, and this seems like a relationship worth cultivating. After asking his name, engaging in some friendly small talk and not a little haggling, an agreement is reached and the trade is completed.

This will be a fine comb for our shopper's son; it has echoes of those great, monumental combs held by the aristocracy only two or three generations ago. Who would have thought that such a gift would ever be within the grasp of this family? The gifted comb is a sign of maturity; its receiver can be expected to consider their personal appearance as an important part of their identity, a message to the world of their status and position in society. As a dress accessory, it will allow its wearer to stand out in public congregation; its ornament, and that elaborate case in which it hangs, will be the envy of many. Upon marriage, the intimacy of the grooming ritual will encourage a tightening of the bond between man and wife, and this connection will become indelibly, if invisibly, inscribed upon the comb itself. The comb should last a lifetime, and – who knows – beyond. It may be passed on to a son or daughter, friend or kinsman, or, perhaps, as was the custom in days gone by, it may even go with its owner into the next life. The opportunities are diverse, but the comb brings with it a repertoire of social and symbolic references, a code that may be read, adapted, or transformed, but cannot be ignored.

This story is, of course, based upon little more than informed speculation. As traditionally viewed by historians and archaeologists (who tend to focus on either individuals in the former case, or material objects in the latter), such a story could be broken down into two distinct narratives:

one of people, and one of things. However, I suggest that these stories are not actually separable, but are rather entangled: a complex meshwork of people, animals, places and objects. By looking at these relations from a variety of perspectives (following the paths and narratives of particular people, objects, or places) we can look at the particularities of the life of a specific 'agent', but can also consider the ways in which it interconnects, and affects other 'players', giving us a unique window onto past society. In this book we will do just that; we will take a look at the Viking Age through the 'eyes' of one particular form of object: the hair comb. This may seem an odd choice; combs do not leap to the front of the mind when most people think about Vikings. Nonetheless, hair is central to the popular images of the 'Viking warrior' (see for instance, fig. 1). Moreover, as we will see, combs are very familiar to the archaeologist, and were certainly important to people in the Viking Age, even if they have been overlooked in popular accounts in television, film and literature.

1. The classic Viking. (Image courtesy Jim Glazzard and Catriona Glazzard, Asgard Crafts)

Viking-Age Europe was, in many ways, a world very different to our own: a world of violence and magic, swords and slaves.[1] But it is important that we don't over-mythologise the period; though very different to our own, there was of course a much more ordinary, 'everyday' side to life in the Viking Age. People made things and traded them; they tended crops and livestock; they cooked and looked after their homes; they drank, gambled and went to market. The streets of Viking York or Dublin would have been lined with beggars, thieves and prostitutes, and yet alive with the sounds of children playing, builders working and merchants selling their wares.

Much has been written about the key historical events of the Viking Age, and about the activities of the royalty and aristocracy, often based upon documents written by the clergy, or extrapolated back from the sagas, written centuries later in Iceland. Similarly, much has been said about the structures and organisation of Viking-Age society and economy, using the evidence of settlement excavations, coinage and dramatic finds such as swords and treasure hoards. However, though lip service is often paid to it, Viking studies have seen far less consideration of the day-to-day activities of ordinary people: a subject most easily accessed through the study of commonplace objects and the roles they play in the structuring of our lives.[2]

But why should we care about these moments of the banal? What can we possibly hope to gain through the study of such utilitarian hardware, or the inconsequential activities in which they become bound up? Such questions are valid, but have their origins in the historical hegemony of the grand narrative. Many studies of the past are characterised by a concern with great events and great lives, and even those who have most eloquently studied some of our more mundane histories have argued that some small stories are more worthy than others.[3] I would contest this. In the earlier prehistoric world, it has been shown that a concern with the everyday is key to understanding broader social themes in the past, that 'routine itself was caught up in social reproduction'.[4] If we take this point of view, day-to-day activities were not (and *are* not) shaped solely by practical considerations such as the availability and physical properties of raw materials, or the difficulties or risks of travel through particular landscapes. Instead, a role must be found for social attitudes, beliefs, even prejudices. Quotidian existence should not be seen to comprise meaningless toil through the mundanities of function, punctuated by moments of poetic, symbolic enlightenment (the latter being those events and experiences that are often placed into the box marked 'ritual' or 'spirituality'). Rather, those routines that from our perspective may seem rather prosaic and uninteresting – the building and maintenance of a house, the manufacture of a tool, the preparation of food, even the use of a comb – may be run through with meaning and symbolism, and are perhaps themselves best characterised as 'ritual'.

Moreover, while we like to imagine the world of the Vikings as one of disorder and chaos, it was in many ways highly structured, and these everyday 'rituals' had to be carried out in the appropriate manner. Thus, there was a right way and a wrong way to make a comb; this we know. But there were also understood rules (perhaps even legislation) regarding the ways in which raw materials could be acquired, and there were implicit agreements about the means by which combs might be exchanged and the venues at which this might take place. All of these understandings were no doubt subject to the shifting influences of politics, economy and social impetus, and thus varied considerably in time and space. Moreover, even the ways in which combs were curated, maintained, used and displayed would have been conditioned by a range of tacit, collectively understood rules and social cues, which were similarly subject to the vicissitudes of fashion and circumstance. It is this collection of almost unfelt influences, an architecture of control that is often explained away as 'common sense', that is the key to understanding the lives of people today, or at any point in the past.

Thus, the study of an 'artefact of the everyday', and the ways in which its biography repeatedly intersects with quotidian existence, provides an invaluable window onto the ways in which the human experience is structured. This is the aim of this book. At the same time, it aims to provide a perspective on the ways in which diverse archaeological, scientific, anthropological and documentary evidence may be brought together to inform and contradict one another, thus allowing the archaeologist to tell engaging and worthy narratives of the past. Our quarry is life in the Viking Age, our medium the humble hair comb.

Why Combs?

Notwithstanding the above, the reasons for a book on a subject as apparently esoteric as Viking haircare may require some clarification. To the archaeologist, early medieval hair combs are familiar and useful artefacts, being relatively frequent, dateable finds from urban excavations in the British Isles and northern Europe. Their lives were much shorter than other forms of material culture (such as buildings), and it has been suggested that they were rarely curated or passed down the family line (though we will come back to this question later in the book).[5] This means that where their styles are easily recognisable, combs make extremely useful archaeological dating tools.

But they are much more than this. They offer great potential for the investigation of patterning in space, as well as time, and if we can read their language, they can speak of travel and trade over short and long distances.

On a more esoteric level, there is the possibility that combs held a variety of meanings beyond the simply practical or hygienic.[6] The use of exotic materials such as ivory may have conferred a certain status upon 'special purpose' combs, while beliefs surrounding deer and antler may even have conditioned attitudes to combs in a more general sense.[7] Moreover, the complex, protracted process of manufacture,[8] together with the elaborate decoration and large size of some combs, and the repair – rather than replacement – of damaged items, is suggestive that some examples, at least, had more symbolic significances, and more interesting lives. Their deliberate, symbolically loaded (perhaps even magical) deposition is therefore of note. In various Scottish contexts they have been found in building 'foundation' or 'sealing' deposits. Furthermore, in early Anglo-Saxon graves, miniature, non-functional combs are known, while more practical examples are frequently interred unburnt with cremated remains.[9] In the furnished burials of the Viking Age they may be found clasped between the hands of the deceased, or in the pelvic region, as if once suspended from a belt.[10] Indeed, a role as a dress accessory seems quite likely; some combs feature ornament on only one face, which would fit well with such a purpose.[11]

Moreover, anthropological, sociological and ethnohistoric data are suggestive of a variety of contexts in which combs may have held special significance. Based upon ethnohistoric analogy,[12] there are suggestions that combs made of exotic materials played a role in gift exchange, while their frequency as carvings in Pictish sculpture is remarkable.[13] In the medieval period, when one might assume that there was a movement towards the functional, combs may have been used in the display of Christian[14] and even mercantile[15] identity. Grooming seems to have had particular associations and connotations of intimacy and personal relationships,[16] while hair itself may have held symbolic meaning. As well as having possible, if somewhat elusive, links with morality, magic and shamanism, hair was bound up with aspects of identity including age, status, gender, religion, ethnicity and group membership, and there may well have been perceived 'rules' about appropriate ways for different people to wear their hair.[17] It is thus possible to see haircare itself as social practice, a sort of technology of appearance.

An Agenda for Study

Having justified the selection of the comb as the medium of our study, it remains to outline the means by which that study will be undertaken. The framework of the book develops out of an approach drawn from anthropology, an approach referred to as the 'biography of objects'.

Though arguably problematic in detail, this piece of theoretical apparatus has much potential in medieval archaeology, and is frequently alluded to but rarely carried through effectively. The technique is herein applied as a framing device as much as an analytical tool, and it serves us well at this point to outline the approach in a little detail.

The basic idea is that we attempt to reach an understanding of the 'lifeways' of an object, and the ways in which these intersect with, influence and are coloured by relationships with people, places and other objects.[18] The many moments of an object's life (which may include, but should not be reduced to, phases of manufacture, trade, consumption and deposition) may all affect the way in which an artefact is conceived and represented in social discourse. Further, as an object passes between owners, becomes worn, patinated, marked, damaged, cleaned or repaired, or is engaged with in different social settings, so the ways in which it is thought of and treated undergo perpetual transformation and manipulation. It therefore follows that, while we are dependent upon the availability of data relating to all the significant phases of an object's life (its production, distribution, use and disposal), this is in itself insufficient. In order to write effective biographies, we need more than detailed analyses of objects themselves; the fundamentals are an understanding of context, and an appreciation of the social situations in which certain symbolic resonances become relevant. We therefore need to bring into focus the myriad ways in which an artefact's biography intersects with those of other animate and inanimate actors. Such an approach should follow the networks of connections with phenomena beyond the artefact itself – animals, buildings, places, people and other animals – and thus need not be linear.

So, how does this work for our combs? Given their uses beyond simple grooming (which, as we will see, is not in itself easy to explain away as empty of meaningful content), combs are not quite as easy to pigeonhole or explain as one may at first think. Thus, in order to fully understand the role they played in Viking-Age society, we have to attempt to perceive them as more than static objects. That is to say that we must try to understand the complexities of their changing meanings, associations and relationships with other items of material culture, people and events. As we have seen, in order to write such object biographies, it is necessary to have information – either by direct observation or through analogy – for all the significant phases of an object's life; its production, distribution, consumption and disposal. Is this, then, an achievable goal?

Traditional archaeological analyses of raw material use and methods of manufacture, together with investigations of use-wear and depositional context, furnish us with some of the data necessary for the useful and instructive construction of biographies. However, in order that combs may properly reveal their potential for illuminating human behaviour and social interaction, we need to progress beyond description, and consider the ways in which we may access the human experience itself. This means moving beyond a study of the comb in its own right, instead focusing on related contextual and 'environmental' data.

In broad terms, it is possible to say a little about the means by which combmakers acquired their raw materials, but to do this we must reach outside of archaeology and consider also the documentary record, ethnography, animal ethology and behaviour, and the study of landscape, vegetation and geomorphology. In particular, it is key that we take full account of the diversity of sources from which raw materials could be acquired, and the disparate landscapes in which they were sought. Thanks to decades of archaeological and experimental enquiry, basic methods of comb manufacture are relatively well understood, and, depending upon date and economic context, we may make reasonable suggestions as to distribution mechanisms. Data relating to use is less accessible, but inference may be drawn from the evidence of wear and repair, while means of disposal is often discernible if combs are recovered *in situ*. Nonetheless, the processes, discourses, events and associations that informed each stage of a comb's life often remain ambiguous.

Thus, the approach taken in this book is one of shifting scales and frames of reference. We will begin by considering whether we can propose any generalities regarding the ways in which the lives of combs operated in Viking-Age Europe. We will then attempt to identify some of the dimensions of variation upon which the stages of a comb's biography may be contingent, and we will use selected case studies in order to demonstrate some of the details of relationships between people, combs, places and things. At all times it should be clear that our aim is to use the comb as a lens through which to consider human experience in Viking-Age Europe; the comb is the medium, not the subject of analysis.

Scope of the Study

Grooming implements have probably been a key component of material culture ever since (if not before) humans were first able to manufacture tools. The use of complex, composite combs of bone and antler has a shorter history, but in Europe the form was particularly popular in the period between the last gasps of the Roman Empire (*c.* fourth century AD) and the later Middle Ages (*c.* fifteenth century, though in England such combs dropped out of fashion soon after the eleventh). In this book, our interest is the Viking Age (*c.* AD 800–1050). Evidence from this era indicates the existence of significant diversity in the ways in which combs were manufactured, traded and used, but the period nonetheless constitutes an interesting analytical unit; the period is characterised by a remarkable degree of long-range travel and trade, and while it does see an increase in the production capacity of certain crafts, the industrial-scale production of combs had yet to begin. It thus allows us to ask interesting questions about the manufacture and meaning of these items at a key point in the development of both industry and social practice.

In terms of geography, the study is primarily concerned with the British Isles, but casts its net wide, incorporating a number of case studies from the Scandinavian homeland. This fosters an appreciation of the diverse ways in which people engaged with this particular piece of material culture. Not all 'Vikings' were the same. Nonetheless, many of the themes discussed will be of interest to archaeologists working on similar material elsewhere in the 'Viking world', from the south coasts of the Baltic, to Iceland and Greenland in the west, and the fringes of Russia in the east.

In accordance with its aims, the volume adopts a biographical structure. Thus, in Chapter 2 we consider the diverse beginnings of combmaking: the varied means by which combmakers acquired their raw materials – the antlers of red deer, reindeer, and elk – and the ways in which the lives and behaviours of the animals themselves in some way placed their influence upon the lives of combs and combmakers. In Chapter 3, we consider the experience of manufacture itself, the choices open to the combmaker and the ways in which this highly specialised technology may be seen to be about far more than simple efficiency, but is in many ways socially embedded. We'll also grapple with the knotty problem of the combmaker's lifestyle, and how this affected the craft itself. Drawing upon anthropology and sociology as well as iconographic, documentary and archaeological evidence, Chapter 4 considers why people *need* combs at all, by questioning the motivation behind personal grooming: is it really as simple and straightforward a business as it seems on the surface to be? Chapter 5 builds on this discussion in considering the diverse uses to which a comb may have been put, as well as the social contexts and intended audiences for such behaviour. In Chapter 6, we consider just some of the possible ends that befell Viking-Age combs, with an eye to what this may say about the societies in which such phenomena persisted. Throughout, the reader will note an emphasis on the relationship between the comb and the communities within which it was situated: communities of artisans, of owners, of observers and objects. These are our real quarry. Our first item of business relates to the search for materials, a search that will take us beyond the urban environments introduced above, and into the woodlands, wetlands and mountains that lay beyond.

2

Beginnings

...people who find antlers which have been left behind in glades, as if they were pledges for future spoils, may adopt them for their own use; but even so, it is no easier to light upon these than it is to mark the calving of the hinds, or the free wild ass bellowing in the barren land.

Olaus Magnus[1]

It begins with deer. Combs may be fashioned from the longbones of horses, cows or sheep, from cattlehorn or tortoisehell, or from the ivory of elephant or walrus, but in the Viking Age the preferred material was deer antler. The materials from which objects are made have a significant influence on the ways in which such objects are used, and even conceived.[2] It thus serves us well to spend a little time considering antler as a material.

Antlers are, of course, the bony cranial outgrowths distinctive to deer (the horns of animals such as cattle, antelope, rhino, etc. are keratinaceous materials; they are also of great use to humans, but are not considered in detail herein).[3] In all species but reindeer, antlers are limited to males. They are grown rapidly each year (ahead of the annual rut), and are ultimately shed after this event. Though broadly synchronous, the precise rate and timing of the antler cycle varies from species to species, and, as we shall see, this has implications for the ways in which humans have been able to exploit this material resource.

As a material, antler is a specialised form of bone; one that is formed rapidly, and in such a way that it will better withstand shocks and physical impacts than other bone.[4] It also has a distinctive structure; if you were to cut a cross section through the middle of an antler beam, you would see that it consists of a ring of hard, dense, compact bone, formed around a core of much more spongy, porous material. This structure, together with the physical properties outlined above, of course allows antler to withstand the intense stresses and impacts of the rut. However, it also imparts on the material certain qualities that allow people to work it in interesting ways. Compact antler is strong, flexible and holds great potential for the manufacture of objects, while the spongy material presents many more problems. As we will see, these fundamentally biological qualities of the material are key influences on the development of combcraft, every bit as important as more 'technological' or 'anthropogenic' considerations. In particular, though the tensile properties of antler mark it out as the perfect, hard-wearing material for use in a comb, the morphological characteristics of antler make it far from easy to work. The relatively thin expanses of useable compact material, coupled with the need to cut teeth with the 'grain' of the antler,[5] mean that combs had to be made of a large number of small pieces, individually riveted together. This ultimately led to the development of the complex, protracted process of manufacture discussed in Chapter 3.

However, as we will see, the material has greater resonance than in either providing a substrate onto which human ideas could be placed or purely constraining the possibilities of human design;[6] it provides potential for choice, it shapes the decisions of the combmaker and it may even presence the deer itself in the objects produced. Thus, if we are to begin to understand the social role played by the manufacture, trade, and use of combs, we must begin with a consideration of the ways in which raw materials were acquired.

It is important to note that just as each of the various deer species have their own lifestyles, patterns of behaviour and habitats, so do their antlers have distinctive physical characteristics and, no doubt, ideological associations. An understanding of these properties and qualities is fundamental to any attempt to characterise the use of the materials and the objects into which they were ultimately transformed. It is thus appropriate to take a little time to consider the behaviour of our various species of interest, with an eye to how this may have influenced the availability and desirability of antler as a raw material. The species that concern us are red deer, reindeer and elk, though we need to be careful with our terminology here; the use of the word 'species' tends to imply the existence of clearly and universally distinguishable animal types. It is arguable whether or not the term has any utility when discussing human attitudes to animals in the past, and there do seem to be examples of medieval observers conflating or confusing red deer and reindeer.[7] However, the behavioural and ethological differences between red deer, reindeer and elk are undeniable, as are the differences in the degree to which, and approach by which, populations may be managed or exploited. Significantly, they also have fairly discrete habitat zones. Thus, for the purposes of discussing the skills and experiences needed in order to harvest antler, our three species are herein considered separately.

We begin with red deer.

Playing the Stag in Viking-Age Britain

Today, the red deer (*Cervus elaphus*, fig. 2) is Britain's largest wild mammal. It is known across much of temperate Europe, with populations in Asia Minor and Africa, as well as more recent introductions to Australasia and South America. In the UK, there are large indigenous populations in Scotland, Exmoor and the Lake District, and more recently established

2. Red deer. (Image by Ruth Carden; drawing by Hayley Saul)

herds in areas such as the New Forest and the Peak District. Beyond the British Isles, red deer are common across much of central, western, and southern Europe, and are also known as far north as western Norway. In order to understand past distributions, however, it is important to appreciate that this range is dynamic rather than fixed. Following the height of the Ice Age, when the distribution contracted into the *refugia* of southern Europe, red deer populations began to expand across Europe, ultimately becoming common right across southern, central and northern Europe (as far as southern Norway and Sweden) by the early Holocene.[8]

North America's 'elk' or 'wapiti' are closely related to the north European red deer, though they are often much larger in size and geneticists now think of them as discrete species. Like other cervids, as well as cattle and pigs, red deer are *artiodactyls* (they have hooves, and an even number of toes) and *ruminants* (meaning that they have a four-chambered stomach and process food through a process of ingestion and regurgitation: 'chewing the cud'). Though we are used to seeing them in parks and on open hillsides, their natural habitat is provided by woodland, and prior to England's extensive late medieval and early modern deforestation, they could be found throughout the British Isles. Red deer are most active in the twilight hours of dusk and dawn, at which times they seem to follow reasonably predictable movements: Scottish populations have been seen to move to lower ground at night and higher ground during the day.[9]

The red deer is an easily recognised member of the north European fauna. Its size, red-brown summer coat and the antlers and manes that distinguish males of the species are instantly distinctive. However, the species shows considerable variation across its geographic range, with particularly marked differences in antler size and overall body dimensions. In Europe, there is something of a north-west–south-east size cline, with British animals considerably smaller and with less substantial antlers than those in Hungary, for instance; this may well be due to the relative lack of available nutrition in the former, particularly among hillside populations.[10] The female red deer (or 'hind') lacks antlers, and is considerably smaller than the male ('stag' or 'hart'), which stands with its shoulder over 1 metre off the ground, and may weigh hundreds of kilograms. The antlers of north European red deer are distinctive, being straight and unpalmated, with a rough surface texture, and a two- or three-pointed crown at the top. We should note, however, that the detailed structure of red deer antler varies between subspecies, and should be taken into consideration when attempting to reconstruct the ways in which the material may have been exploited for manufacture (Chapter 3). Red deer frequently live until the age of twelve or thirteen, and males reach their prime at around the age of eight, after which their antlers start to 'go back', decreasing in size and complexity from year to year.

One aspect of cervid zoology that is of particular interest is the annual growth, loss and regrowth of antlers; indeed this is perhaps the most distinctive element of the ethology and biology of deer. The timing of this cycle varies between species, but in red deer, new antlers start to develop in the spring, during which time they are protected within a surface coating of velvet. Velvet is lost in autumn, by which point the antlers are fully grown. They are, of course, central to the autumn rut, and are ultimately cast at the end of the winter.

This cycle of growth, loss and regrowth is centred on the mating season, but there are of course other seasonal controls on the behaviour of red deer, such as the availability of food, and the birth and rearing of young. Winter is usually spent in low-lying woodland, but, with the dawn of summer, and the impending birth of new calves, red deer migrate to higher altitudes in search of ground with greater nutritional potential. For much of the year, adult stags congregate together in single-sex 'bachelor' groups; hinds also form large groups. However, come the appearance of their antlers, males become much less gregarious, and in the autumn they begin to compete in what is known as the rut. This ritualised performance comprises stags attempting to attract females, and to retain them as harems, which they then endeavour to defend from other males. Dominant stags will be challenged by other large males, through a combination of choreographed walking and roaring, and ultimately through engaging in a sort of antler-bound trial of strength. The effort invested in maintaining a harem is immense, and these stags rarely eat, meaning that only the strongest survive the season with their harems intact, while weaker stags (including both young and senescent individuals) tend to be confined to the peripheries of the theatre.

During the rut, dominant males will mate with a number of female individuals, often multiple times with a single hind. After a gestation period of around eight months, the result is the late spring/summer birth of a single fawn to each successful female. Though weaned after eight weeks, fawns do not leave their mother's side until the following calving season, and these family groups themselves cluster into much larger herds. Such congregations have the important function of providing protection, both through safety in numbers, and through the employment of particular individuals as 'look-outs'. Today, the key threats to red deer are wolves, and this would also have been the case in the Viking Age, though bears may also have been active in some areas, and small predators such as wildcats and even boar may have constituted a threat to young deer. Of course, we should not forget the significance of human predation; stag hunting as a leisure pursuit has been central to the maintenance of elite and aristocratic identity for a thousand years,[11] while the hunting of deer for food and secondary products has a history of many millennia.

Relations of Encounter

An understanding of the phenomena outlined above would be fundamental in any attempt to extract resources from red deer, whether by means of hunting or collection of cast antlers. While the points of reference and explanations of animal behaviour may have been strikingly different to our own (see for instance accounts of cervid appearance and ethology in Pliny's *Natural History*, or the later medieval bestiaries), a heightened awareness of movement, of sensation, of landscape – a kind of animal empathy – would have been essential to anyone attempting to follow the herd.[12]

To put that another way, tracking relies on a canon of experiential knowledge about deer. On a basic level, one must understand the habitats in which these animals live, and their patterns of seasonal migration. One must be similarly familiar with seasonal changes in behaviour: when are males most likely to be found huddled together in large groups, and when will they be patrolling the landscape in relative isolation? Such knowledge has to work on a range of scales: at what times of the day are the deer most active? When are they most wary, most vulnerable? And more specific local knowledge is also key: where are the preferred watering holes, patches of vegetation, woodland or scrub? What do their tracks and pellets look like, where might one find them and how can they be read? What are the tell-tale signs of rubbing vegetation, for either the removal of antler velvet, or moulting of the winter coat?

Red deer can be dangerous animals; stags should be avoided during the rut, as should hinds minding their young. They are also fleet of foot and keenly aware of the threat of predation, with highly attuned senses of smell and hearing, while their eyes are well adapted to the recognition of movement, even in low light. An awareness of these traits constitutes the base level of requisite knowledge for any stalker, but might one even become familiar with the behaviour of particular individuals? Are some deer more frisky, nervous, or aggressive than others? All such considerations need to be taken into account if the deer is to be successfully stalked.

It is worth reiterating that such skilled knowledge is fundamental not only to hunting, but also to the collection of shed antler.[13] This material seems, in many cases, to have been central to the production of composite combs in the Viking Age (antler-bases from deposits of working waste at sites across northern Europe are dominated by examples from shed antler, rather than butchered material, though Novgorod in north-western Russia is an exception), and its collection must have been dependent upon a relationship with the deer, one borne out of close observation of the herd, and of individuals, over several years.[14] Antler, shed in late winter, will quickly decay in the wild, as it undergoes physical and microbial attack at the hands (or rather, teeth) of rodents, the elements, even sheep and other deer.[15] Thus, the collector must closely observe the animals, in order to anticipate the first casting of material. Commentators as far back as Olaus Magnus (see above) have bemoaned the difficulty of finding antler in the wild; it is not a simple case of wandering around the countryside, picking up materials as you find them.[16] Stags tend to shed their antlers in relative solitude, so one is unlikely to find large numbers of beams lying closely together. Rather, one must learn how to trace the movements of deer, and to identify the geomorphological and floral signs that indicate a likely spot for casting. This is a task for the skilled tracker: a wayfarer firmly rooted in the local environment, their senses finely attuned to the physical, faunal and floral contours of place. These are not skills passed on via books, but through verbal communication, and, more importantly, through experience, and physical engagement in key activities.[17]

Discussions of contemporary deerstalking and antler-collecting practice may be enlightening in this regard.[18] These accounts demonstrate the importance of a surprisingly wide repertoire of skills and 'silent knowledge'[19]. Thus, as well as an understanding of landscape and animal behaviour, the stories of contemporary collectors evidence the importance of a familiarity with local climate, and of an understanding of the optimal weather conditions for the exercise. For instance, North American followers of white-tailed deer (*Odocoileus virginianus*) have noted that antlers tend to be found more tightly clustered together in harsh winters, as the search for nutrition and shelter forces together animals otherwise predisposed to dispersal. Further, beginning the search in late winter improves chances of success, as the spring vegetation has not yet started to build to an extent that makes it difficult to trace (or physically follow) the tracks of their quarry. Nonetheless, it is important to wait until the cessation of freezing precipitation, as snow-covered ground renders antlers near invisible, while grasses and ground plants recently freed of its weight will be pressed flat, making it much easier to spot the object of one's endeavours. Finally, the task of collection is rendered more difficult as the bright, late winter sun generates a frustrating panorama of shadows (particularly when walking into the sun), whereas overcast skies provide the perfect conditions for 'antler spotting'.

These present-day collectors of course emphasise the importance of attention to detail, and familiarity with the signs of cervid activity. For instance, shed antlers are frequently associated with 'lays': flattened areas of grass or vegetation formed by the deer's repose in rest or sleep, while other indicators of activity might include signs of feeding, such as leaves stripped from vegetation, or the presence of a distinctive 'browse line' at deer height. The stripping of velvet involves vigorous rubbing of antlers on the trunks of trees; this leaves a very clear indication that deer were at least in this region earlier in the year, while rough undergrowth might preserve the evidence of an individual having passed through, in the form of caught hair. Finally, searching the ground may reveal evidence of recent activity, such as 'scrapes', produced by the pounding of earth with the hooves – a particular common behavioural trait in the rutting season – as well as footprints and droppings.

However, in addition to an ability to recognise these 'tells', contemporary hunters, trackers, and collectors also note the importance of an ability to read the landscape, as this allows the location of watering holes, browse and areas of escape-cover that may not be immediately apparent to the human eye, but which nonetheless draw the attention of deer. Also key is a degree of empathy: a willingness to attempt to adopt the deer's perspective, and to consider, for instance, where deer might shelter from the elements. This allows the search to be focused in river valleys, on south-facing slopes with good browse, in long grasses and in areas of light woodland that allow the heat of the sun to penetrate and to stimulate the growth of ground and low-level vegetation.

Other landscape phenomena are important too; anything that forces the deer to jump, or make other sudden, exaggerated movements may catalyse antler loss. Thus, ditches and waterways are productive places to search. Regarding the latter, deer are more likely to find crossing points in the straight stretches of streams, as the banks here are shallower than at the bends, providing another mechanism by which the search might be narrowed. Such an approach leads to a largely instinctual feel for the topography and vegetation (both in terms of density and species composition) that 'attracts' antlers. Deer may regularly return to these spots, and thus they should also be revisited by the collector. Indeed, retreading the same ground can often lead to the identification of antlers missed on previous traverses. In this regard, it is interesting to note that contemporary experience suggests that the potential for successful antler collection is increased when it is undertaken as a team exercise, rather than a solitary pursuit, and that children have a particular eye for the task.[20] Finally, having considered the various factors that enable the collector to carefully identify the areas in which they might best focus their search, and the most appropriate conditions for that search, we must not overlook the degree to which the ability to *see* is in itself a practised technology. The experienced collector will be able to pick out the glint of a slightly polished tine tip among a mass of leaves and heather, or the rugose texture of an antler beam against the bark of a dead tree. The novice, quite simply, will not. In all, the collection of shed antler does not constitute the leisurely pursuit of an afternoon, but the focused efforts of an experienced hand and eye.

While these observations have their genesis in a context very different to the environment of early medieval northern Europe, and the species of interest also differs from the quarry of the Viking-Age collector, in many ways the details are unimportant. For our purposes, what is significant is the fact that successful collecting develops out of a very specific form of expertise, a kind of *technology* of collection (*cf.* Chapter 3), and that this in itself emerges from a practical engagement with the task, through articulation of the mind, body and senses, in a particular place and over an extended period of time.

Thus, one may hazily perceive the existence of a particular form of relationship between humans and deer, a relationship borne out of unwavering focus on the part of the human, out of observation and encounter, if not with the animals themselves, then with their tracks.[21] It is inconceivable that Viking-Age antler collectors failed to appreciate the relationship between living deer and the antlers that constitute material traces of their presence; even if shedding was rarely observed in person, an understanding of where this material came from is fundamental to the ability to efficiently locate it in the landscape. This was not a case of stumbling across unexplained natural resources in the landscape (though that may have been how it began), but rather one based on an understanding of, respect for, even affinity with the deer. One may conceive of the stories that may have been told of the ways in which antlers came to be lost, of the theories espoused as to the reasons for the existence of such a strange phenomenon as the antler cycle. Indeed, as we have seen, medieval bestiaries and religious texts provide some insight into the circuitous lines of thought employed in order to make sense of this natural marvel, but we should be careful not to assume identity between such literary rationale and explanations based upon more everyday encounters with deer, on local knowledge and experience.

So, given that there was a demand for antler in the workshops of Viking-Age Europe, and that collection of this material was dependent on a certain degree of talent and no little experience, we may postulate that the collection of antler was a recognised pursuit at the time. With its fundamentally seasonal character, it cannot have constituted a full-time occupation, but may have been an important endeavour in the late winter and early spring. Questions remain as to how this activity may have been pursued, the degree to which access to land was controlled and whether there were any restrictions on the right to extract this resource.

It is of course possible that combmakers themselves engaged in antler collection for part of the year. If this was the case, then they must have had well-defined homebases and catchment areas, as they would need to be familiar with local landscape and the movement of deer. An alternative suggestion is that members of local communities curated something of a stockpile, which they could supply to craftworkers and artisans when they came to market within some generally understood arrangement of mutual exchange, perhaps controlling the price of material according to time of year and concomitant reduction in availability.[22] This may perhaps have been operable in some regions (see below), but it hardly seems the most efficient solution in areas in which red deer provided the source of antler; how could a travelling combmaker be sure that the necessary materials would be present at any given market, or that they could be acquired at a workable cost? This question has implications for the organisation of combmaking itself, which we will return to in Chapter Three, but for now, we must retain focus on the issue of material collection and storage. There are important logistical concerns we have not yet considered: once collected, how would antler have been protected from decay? Where would it have been stockpiled? Are we to envision antler storehouses of some form?

Given these requirements, it is perhaps more likely that there was some organised structure of resource control and distribution, rather than such trade being in the hands of diverse townspeople and subject to rather *ad hoc* arrangements of collection, storage, and exchange. Such a model is consistent with the need for the involvement of skilled trackers and wayfarers, discussed above. Furthermore, given what we know of the elite associations of deer in the Viking Age, and the increasingly dogmatic Anglo-Norman restrictions later placed upon access to, and engagement with, deer, one might posit that any such structured network of collection and supply may have been organised through the managers of aristocratic estates.[23] Antler may have been collected under the aegis of the local lord, by someone familiar with the landscape, flora and fauna of his estate; perhaps even a gamekeeper or forester of some sort.[24] Certainly, recent studies have highlighted a Viking-Age trend towards certain social practices (such as hunting) and their associated landscapes becoming 'closed off' to all but the elite.[25] More specifically, a law of Cnut (King of England between AD 1016 and 1035) legislates against hunting on his 'preserves'; the enforcement of any such arrangement surely presupposes the existence of some sort of warden.

Alternatively, given the analogy of contemporary practice, we may propose that the task was undertaken in groups, perhaps even family groups.[26] Whoever was responsible for collection on the ground, material could then be securely stockpiled, no doubt with other valuable and tradeable goods. The antler might then be maintained for the use of artisans indentured to the lord in the production of commissions (particularly in the early Viking Age), or supplied to the more independent combmakers that populated the urban markets of the tenth and eleventh centuries. It may even have been exchanged with some form of middleman ahead of sale at market, or a merchant who could take the material (once properly processed into a transportable cargo) further afield. Such a transfer must have been mediated through sale, indentured service or the levying of some form of tax. Unfortunately, documentary sources are silent on this issue, and all we are able to do is speculate as to which of the various possible scenarios seems most likely.

Tracking Elk in Viking-Age Sweden

The behaviour, ethology, and antler morphology of European elk (*Alces alces*, 'moose' in North America) differs considerably from that of both reindeer and red deer, and thus presents rather a different challenge for those collecting, and working with, its antler. They are the largest of the deer species (at up to 2 metres high at the shoulder, by some margin), but even so their antlers are inordinately large and palmated, and are distinguished from those of most other deer by the fact that they protrude from the sides – rather than the top – of the head (fig. 3).

Today their range includes much of subarctic and temperate Scandinavia and northern Russia, with smaller populations in the areas to the immediate south and east of the Baltic, as well as Canada, and the

3. Elk. (Image by Ross Docherty; drawing by Hayley Saul)

northernmost states of the USA. Its European range is but a shadow of its prehistoric and antique extent: at the end of the Roman era, elk would have been recognisable components of the local fauna across much of northern Europe, but by the start of the Viking Age this had contracted substantially, with the last populations probably disappearing from the Netherlands by the tenth century, though they persisted a little longer in central Europe. In terms of habitat, elk are quite adaptable, and may be found in temperate valleys, floodplains, taiga and tundra landscapes, but their ideal environment (and the niche they very largely occupy in Scandinavia) is in deciduous forests of spruce and pine. Here, they feed largely on flowering plants, tree shoots and water lilies, and benefit from the fresh growth of vegetation that follows fires, floods, and other disturbances of tree cover.[27] In the summer, they are to be seen in marshy and riverine environments, where they often wade into water for respite from heat and insects.

Elk behaviour differs a little from that of our other species, which brings its own particular challenges for the antler collector (see below). They are most active during the daylight hours, and are largely solitary animals. They do not tend to congregate in groups outside of the mating season, being most commonly spotted either in isolation, or in mother-calf pairs. Elk antlers begin to grow under velvet in springtime, ahead of the autumn rut, and they are subsequently shed (usually sometime around January). Calves are born in late spring, and may stay with their mother for up to a year.

Elk are long-lived animals; many may live for twenty years. Other than man, their greatest predatory threats come from wolves and bears, though they are less easily brought down by wolves than are other deer species. Humans have hunted elk for thousands of years; prior to the availability of guns, this was undertaken primarily through the use of pit traps. There is good reason for their exploitation in this way. Other than antlers, the elk produces meat and skins, though it should be noted that its kidneys and liver are high in cadmium – potentially dangerously so.

Relations of Encounter
One might suppose that the experience of tracking the European elk would share certain commonalities with red deer stalking, though the task is in many ways even more difficult, given the fact that elk spend much of the year in a solitary existence. Similarly, hunters have noted that the elk presents a number of particular challenges to the stalker. In addition to their isolated existence and low population density, they are able to move rapidly over rough ground, have very thick hides, and are known to attack hunters. Thus, even when located, they may evade

predation through flight, resilience, aggression, or any combination thereof.[28] Nonetheless, the principles remain the same; an awareness of the behaviour, movements and predispositions of the animal, as well as a close familiarity with local topography, flora, fauna and weather, and an eye for the traces of movement all combine to maximise the chance of success. Finding one antler may lead the collector to redouble efforts to locate its pair, though there is of course no guarantee that this will lie close by. On the other hand, in particularly harsh winters elk are known to congregate in restricted areas characterised by superior browse, which can lead to multiple finds. In detail, there is less written on the act of following the elk than there is on running with red deer or reindeer, but one might expect to search in areas close to water, to identify areas of undergrowth disturbed by recent rutting, to look in the trees for the very distinctive signs of velvet removal, at young vegetation for signs of browsing, and on the ground for 'lays' and for their large, round pellets and stools. The collector learns from their experiences year on year, but again the technique of seeing the landscape from the animal's point of view seems to be important – a sort of heightened sensory awareness borne out of some level of empathy.[29]

Modern collectors tend to search in winter, when the presence of elk tracks in snow allows an easier path to the freshly fallen antlers. The climate at this time of year also means that many waterways and wetlands are frozen, thus easing travel, while the collector will also be spared the nuisance of the spring's biting insects. We might expect our Viking-Age collectors to have developed similar strategies. Nonetheless, given the behaviour and habitat of the elk, the search for their antlers must still have been long and arduous, and, on occasion, not a little dangerous, but the rewards must have been considerable. The elk's large, palmate antlers (the largest known span is almost 2 metres) yield long, broad areas of workable, compact material, and just a single antler would provide a resource sufficient for the production of several combs. Moreover, given the quality and scarcity of the source, one might expect such materials to be at an economic premium, whether in the world of reciprocal or market exchange. Given the low density of elk populations, and the fact that for much of the animal's life its antlers increase in size year on year, one might suppose that there would be certain advantages to knowing the movements of a particular individual, and it is not out of the question that particular animals were targeted for this purpose, informally tracked over the course of the year, before their antlers were ultimately harvested in the annual collection. This presents a slightly different scenario to those proposed for either red deer or reindeer; we are not talking here of the control of access to land and resources that characterised Anglo-Norman (and perhaps Viking-Age) England. Nor are we considering the trapping of individuals within large herds, or the maintenance of those herds as semi-domestic livestock. Instead, I envision certain skilled trackers focusing their attention on particular areas of landscape – perhaps even on particular individuals within wild populations – in order to effectively acquire an invaluable resource. It is of course possible (even likely?) that this material became the property of, or its circulation subject to control at the hands of, the elite, and that some form of levy was extracted upon its trade. This is impossible to know, but we can say that the material itself found its way to the combmaker, and was collected by an individual with specialised skills and knowledge. Whether it is correct to speak of this tracker as a specialist *per se*, is more difficult; clearly they undertook other activities between late spring and midwinter. Nonetheless this was something that they engaged in on an annual basis; they knew the value of it, and took it seriously.

Notwithstanding the low population density of elk, the species does seem to be quick to recover from over-predation, even in the modern era.[30] It would therefore be foolhardy to rule out the possibility of their antlers reaching combmakers via hunting. It all depends on the ease with which elk antler could be found, and thus how reliable a source it was. Nonetheless, given the success of modern-day collectors, we should certainly not discount the possibility of shed collection playing an important role in the supply of raw materials to the comb trade. Trapping was certainly another option, and it is interesting to note that in the Døvre region, associations of large pitfalls have been found, arranged across the ridge-valley lines (rather than along them, as was the case for reindeer).[31] These trap alignments have been interpreted as evidence of an attempt to intercept and catch elk on their short seasonal migrations. However, it is interesting to note that elk antlers are shed in January, and this coincides with the time at which the fur of many northern animals (such as squirrel) is at its thickest. It is thus possible that hunters were collecting elk antler while trapping much smaller prey.[32] Indeed, the potential for a combination of activities is considerable.

Nonetheless, whether stalking, trapping or collection provided the primary mechanism by which elk antler was harvested, it should be said that the relative scarcity of this material and the problems associated with its acquisition do not seem to have been a bar to its use; Birka in particular provides copious evidence for its exploitation, in the form of both waste and combs. Moreover, though prehistorians have claimed it is difficult to work,[33] this does not seem to have prevented its exploitation on some scale in the Viking Age. The material is, indeed, very tough, but with the right tools (see Chapter 3), it provides greater expanses and thicknesses of useable compact antler than other species, thus facilitating the manufacture of longer, broader, flatter and more uniformly shaped combs (and in many cases it allowed more combs to be produced from a single antler) than was the case for either red deer or reindeer.

Thus, the scarcity of elk antler, together with its relatively high working potential (in the right hands) may well have added to its appeal. In the ninth and early tenth centuries, for example, many large, ornate combs seem to have been manufactured in elk antler and it has been suggested that this form could only really have developed in elk.[34] Indeed, there are a number of truly monumental examples, for which this would be the only material option. Certainly, the large red deer combs of the British Isles and southern Scandinavia cannot compete in terms of regularity or overall aesthetic with examples known from areas such as Sweden and the Netherlands, where elk would have been indigenous, and where there is evidence for their exploitation. Thus, it may be that something of a market developed for elk antler; this was a material that facilitated the production of large, exquisite items, and which thus became prized in its own right, just as was ivory in nineteenth-century Europe.

'Following' Reindeer in Viking-Age Norway

Our final species of interest is the reindeer (*Rangifer tarandus*, fig. 4). Known in North America as 'caribou', the exploitation of reindeer presents very different challenges and possibilities to those encountered in the above studies of red deer and elk. A native of the Arctic and subarctic, populations are known to have existed right across Scandinavia, northern

4. Reindeer. (Image by Alex Smith, Cairngorm Reindeer Centre; drawing by Hayley Saul)

Russia, China, North America and Greenland, where they exploit both the barren expanses of the tundra and the coniferous forests of the taiga. The southern part of their range is now very much diminished,[35] but in the Viking Age, populations would have been known throughout the northern stretches of Europe and western Russia.

Reindeer of course share many similarities with other members of the deer family (see above), but a few differences are significant, primarily evolving as adaptations to the cold climate they inhabit. Like red deer, their senses of smell and hearing are acute, while their eyesight is primarily attuned to movement. Also like other cervids, they have a four-chambered stomach, but are able to persist on a diet heavy in lichen, rather than grass. Nonetheless, their diet necessarily varies according to seasonal availability, and they may also eat sedges, fungus, heather, brushwood and leaves.[36] Like red deer, they mate in autumn, with males once again engaging in competition for the right to mate, and – in Scandinavian populations at least – to build a harem. Calves are born in late spring, and thereafter continue to suckle for an extended period (as late as September), in order to build up sufficient strength for survival in the harsh environment.

In terms of physical adaptations, reindeer have thick pelts, specialised noses and hooves, and large antlers with 'snow shovels' close to the base. A key distinction that sets reindeer apart from all other cervids is the fact that both males and females grow antlers. This is thought to be related to the fact that they live together in much larger – and hence more competitive – herds than other deer. The fact that females retain antlers until the birth of their young in late Spring or early summer (while males shed around October, immediately after the rut), means that the former may attain a kind of winter dominance, and are able to command priority over browse; at the very least the presence of antlers allows them to more effectively dig for vegetation.[37] Females (cows) are nonetheless easily distinguishable from mature males (bulls), on account of the very much greater size of antlers in the latter.

However, one phenomenon characteristic of northern climes, and to which the reindeer does not seem to be perfectly adapted, is the nuisance of biting insects and other parasites. Reindeer hides and noses may become subject to the deposition of fly larvae, leading to severe infestation, while the summer appearance of mosquitoes and blackflies can cause severe anxiety. It is thus notable that when temperatures are at their highest, reindeer herds tend to pack together and move up to higher ground, into areas where food is less plentiful, but where the wind provides a sufficient coolant to discourage an insect following. Such environments also help reindeer themselves to cool, as they have few sweat glands.[38] On a broader canvas, small reindeer populations come together in search of winter forage, forming herds in the tens or hundreds of thousands for the trek to the taiga, before breaking into smaller groups for the mating season, and returning to calving grounds in the spring.

With regard to their exploitation at the hands of humans, these behaviours are of particular note. The reindeer's predispositions to the formation of herds, and to large-scale movements, constitute the key behavioural differences between *Rangifer* and red deer. Indeed, reindeer may aggregate together into very large herds, and may travel hundreds of miles annually. These aggregations provide protection from such diverse predators as wolves, bears, wolverine and birds of prey, who obviously see the migrating, breeding caravan as something of a walking larder, but it is notable that even forest-dwelling reindeer (see below) still maintain reasonably large herd sizes, notwithstanding the cover provided by the presence of woodland.[39]

At this juncture, it is necessary to note that not all reindeer are alike in either physical morphology or behaviour. There are many subtle differences between populations, but for our purposes it is sufficient to note the existence of two broad sub-groups: the *tundra reindeer* and the *woodland reindeer*.[40] *Woodland reindeer* are large, and notably less gregarious than their tundra conspecifics. Their migrations are relatively restricted in scope, consisting simply of movements between valleys and uplands.[41] *Tundra reindeer* are generally smaller, and are predisposed to group together in herds of exceptionally large size (upwards of 200,000 individuals in some North American cases), making them particularly susceptible to overtures toward domestication. Their migrations occur on a scale altogether more grand than that of the woodland reindeer, every spring travelling distances that may be in the hundreds of kilometres from the forests to the tundra, where their young will be born and the summer will be spent, before returning to the forest in the autumn. Migration routes are not annually consistent, but rather the precise destinations and the means by which they are reached are subject to change year on year.[42]

Relations of Encounter

To the degree to which they are understood, these characteristics of reindeer behaviour – aggregation and migration – have conditioned human responses to, and relationships with, the animals. In parts of northern Scandinavia, Finland, and Russia, thousand-strong groups of semi-domesticated reindeer are systematically managed and exploited by Saami herders (see Glossary), while the exploitation of reindeer as a wild resource is also well documented. The fact that these animals are able to support such diverse tactics of exploitation makes them a rather challenging subject of archaeological enquiry, and the history of reindeer hunting, trapping, and herding is thus worth spending some time on here.

As a premise from which to begin our discussion, we can do worse than to open with the statement that reindeer populations are difficult to find.[43] Notwithstanding the fact that herds may number in the thousands at certain times of year, the taiga and tundra are vast, and, as we have seen, a herd's seasonal movements are not predictable in detail. Moreover, the environment is dangerous and resistant to rapid movement for even the most well adapted of animals.[44] It is often thought that past human communities whose survival depended upon the presence of reindeer 'followed' their migrations, though it is now some time since Ernest Burch[45] demonstrated that such an idea was not feasible. It is not possible even for single individuals to match the pace of a migrating herd over any distance, and even if it were, any benefits derived from the capture and slaughter of animals would hardly repay the necessary energy investment. Following reindeer is simply not a sustainable mode of existence, with the possible exception of those herds that move over short distances between uplands and valleys. Such a situation does pertain in northern Scandinavia, but even in this case, sustained pursuit would be extremely challenging, could involve only a subset of the population (typically adult males), and would be dependent upon the possession of sleds and animals (perhaps tame reindeer) with which to pull them.[46]

Instead, we might envision an approach described as 'interception', and which makes use of tracking, trapping and ambush, rather than relying on pursuit alone.[47] In this way, rather than following a single herd all year round, the aim is to interrupt their movements at particular moments on the annual circuit. The difference here is key; such an approach allows the 'interceptors' to remain in one place on the 'deerpath' for short periods of time, in order to cache food and other resources, before moving on to the next ambush point. As Ingold cogently points out, the key skill here is not the ability to maintain constant contact with the reindeer, but rather to anticipate their movements and respond in a timely fashion. The survival of a society is dependent upon the collection of sufficiently large yields at key points on the calendar, between which movement is reduced. As is the case for the red deer stalker, such an approach presumes an understanding of both landscape and animal behaviour, but the case here is perhaps even stronger; topography is difficult and unpredictable to the unfamiliar, with rocky outcrops, bogs and watercourses to be negotiated, and of course the greater dangers of snowstorm and avalanche. The hunter would thus need not only tracking and wayfaring expertise, but also a repertoire of survival abilities and a canon of landscape knowledge, such that they were able to navigate to safe routes or find shelter in extreme weather.[48] Important routes would have been marked in the landscape, but the signs (marked in the trees, or on the ground with small piles of stones) could be ephemeral or imperceptible to the uninitiated; aliens wandering mountain Norway would need to be well versed in the Saami language of landscape.

However, in the Adamvalldá valley, northern Norway, a different form of trail has been identified. This pathway, marked by pairs of large, regularly spaced standing stones, has an almost monumental character, and may have been commissioned in order to assist the navigation of Norse traders in the Saami north; it may even perhaps have been intended to announce their presence and authority in the region.[49] Though, in terms of archaeological visibility, the Adamvalldá trail is an unusual phenomenon, documents tell us of Scandinavian traders travelling to the north to trade, particularly in the winter, when they travelled by sled and ski to Saami villages in the taiga. There has been some dispute regarding the nature of Norse–Saami relations,[50] but whether they entailed gift exchange, tax, trade, tribute (i.e. extortion) or combinations of these, it is clear that furs, antler and ivory were important resources to the Saami, and for export as much as for personal use.

Hunting activity in reindeer-hunting societies tends to be focused upon the spring and autumn migrations, when herds tend to spread out into extended columns comprising thousands of individuals, so easing the slaughter of the large numbers that are needed to provide sustenance, particularly over the winter. It is also notable that, given the potential for parasitic infestation to ruin a reindeer hide, the optimum time to harvest the latter is in the late summer and early autumn, before the summer's larvae have fully established themselves in the new coat, and after the perforations caused by the infestations of the previous seasons have healed.[51] We might also note that the antlers of the male red deer will be out of velvet by August, so it is the autumn hunt that is best placed to recover large quantities of antler 'on the head'; by the spring they will have been lost. Collection of shed antler would require a focus on the winter pastures of the valleys and forests, where the benefits of a reduction in reindeer mobility are counterbalanced by reduced aggregation, and the fact that, as antler is shed over an extended period between late December and March, it may be spread over both the winter pastures and along the route down from the mountains.

Hunting: Landscapes and Technologies

Thus, the acquisition of antler as a product (or by-product) of hunting seems the more practical option. As we have seen, the acts of locating a herd and planning an ambush are not in themselves straightforward.

But let us assume that our hunters have successfully identified the path to be taken by a migrating herd. How then do they go about physically bringing down their prey efficiently and effectively? A number of methods have been applied. Key among these is the construction – in advance of the arrival of the herd – of hunting architectures. Arrangements of stone cairns, wooden drift fences or lines of 'flags' or 'deer scarers' are often used to funnel animals towards waiting hunters armed with bows and spears. Variations on this approach are still in operation today, and the use of the technique in antiquity is evidenced by the presence of standing cairns on the plateaux at Hardangervidda and Dovre, and by the preservation in permafrost of deer-scarers in southern Norway's high alpine areas. Ultimately, archers might be secreted in ditches or behind blinds, or the animals might be funnelled into an enclosure, or through snares and trapping pits, rendering them easy targets. Alternatively, the kill might be made at a river crossing, where hunters in canoes and kayaks are able to easily pick off swimming animals. In this regard, it is interesting to note that archaeological study of huts, middens and associated hunting landscapes at Sumtangen, Hardangervidde, has identified large-scale 'mass kills' similar to these more recently recorded events.[52] However, these hunts seem to have been unusual in medieval Scandinavia, and at Sumtangen took place for a relatively short period (no more than fifty years, and possibly considerably less than that) in the thirteenth century. Moreover, they seem to have been organised by outsiders – perhaps for the benefit of the king and archbishops – rather than local hunting populations, although the latter may have been involved in the hunt itself. A proportion of the large quantities of meat, hides and antler gathered in this way seem certain to have been destined for the urban markets of Bergen and (perhaps) Oslo; the scale of Norway's urban combmaking industry at this point is notable. However, there is no suggestion that such intensive hunting strategies were pursued in the Viking Age, and we need not concern ourselves with them here.

Nonetheless, the presence of hunting landscapes, consisting of pit traps and funnel-shaped driveways, do testify to the importance of hunting on a fairly significant scale; the plains of Hardangervidda and Dovre are littered with pit traps and associated camps or settlement sites (complete with middens of reindeer remains) dated to the Viking Age and succeeding century or so.[53] Recent surveys have demonstrated that such traps were consistently arranged not across the hill line, but rather along them, presumably in order to intercept reindeer moving through their migration routes that cross between the hills, high plateaux and valleys.[54]

The choice of technology seems to be largely conditioned by local environment; different structures are built in woodland and open tundra for instance, being governed by raw material availability, space and deer behaviour.[55] However, few of these techniques would be effective were it not for the rapid passage of thousands of reindeer. Thus, when deer products were required outside of the migration seasons, hunting would have taken place on a much more limited scale, and while pitfall traps and snares can be used passively, much small-scale hunting must have taken the form of coursing with sleds, or of lone or paired stalkers, either in disguise or using a tame 'decoy' reindeer as a sort of bait.[56] The same might perhaps be said for cases in which animal selection is important; the passive use of pit traps, for instance, could not guarantee the slaughter of male animals. In practice, however, the most efficient way of ensuring the collection of large numbers of antlered males would probably have been through the use of traps and drives on the autumn migrations; sheer weight of numbers would conspire to guarantee a proportionate kill of males.

Historically, these hunts must have been vital to the survival of many Arctic and subarctic peoples, for whom the reindeer provided the key source of food and secondary products. Large hauls would have been followed by long periods of austerity, so it would have been necessary to kill sufficient animals to provide a store of preserved meat that could see the hunters and their dependants through the winter. The obvious implication of this is that the instincts and readiness of the hunter are key to the survival of the wider human population. As we have seen, reindeer migration routes are subject to annual change, but certain assumptions about likely patterns of movement nonetheless have to be made, and success or failure hangs on the precision of such estimates. Some general rules do seem to apply: migrating reindeer unswervingly follow the trails made by their immediate forerunners, and do seem to follow topographic contours, picking out lines of least resistance along the ridges and valleys of otherwise difficult terrain.[57] However, such a geomorphological awareness is not in itself sufficient. Ease of passage may be influenced not only by topography, but also by factors such as depth and firmness of snow (reindeer seem to prefer soft, undisturbed snow, up to about 0.5 metres thick), and, as we have seen, the nuisance of insects. Moreover, any hunting party would also need to consider the ultimate destination of the herd (whether lowland pasture or exposed highland), its initial degree of dispersion, and such diverse environmental phenomena as temperature, strength and direction of winds.[58] Many of these factors are of course interdependent; the location of concentrations of biting flies, for instance, will be contingent upon local variations in climate and atmospheric temperature,[59] while seasonal changes in snow cover and the availability of food will affect the movement and aggregation of deer.[60] The hunter must tacitly understand such relationships, and accordingly make judgement calls for which there is very little margin for error.

But who were these hunters? We know that the Saami were well established across much of Norway, Sweden and Finland by early in the first millennium AD,[61] and that they were engaging in reindeer hunting well before the start of the Viking Age.[62] It thus serves us well to discuss them in a little detail; they may well turn out to be important actors in the performance of comb production and use.

Hunting and Herding: Saami Lifeways

In the Viking Age, the Saami lifestyle would have broadly followed the pattern recorded in accounts of contemporary arctic 'hunter-gatherer' societies (see above). Their world view was shaped by the landscape they inhabited, and the ways in which they engaged with that environment. That is to say that while we, as western observers, might perceive a division between everyday existence and the worlds of ritual, magic and religion, for our early medieval Saami such a distinction would seem rather alien. Rather, their day-to-day movements and activities, and particularly their subsistence strategies, would have been bound up with stories about the past, hopes for the future and beliefs regarding how to ensure that next year would be better than this.[63] Of course, in all of this, the reindeer was key. As Tim Ingold has said, '[The] power of disposal over a wild animal resource, whose reproduction lies outside human control, is generally vested with the supernatural.' That is to say that successful reindeer hunting is dependent on more than the skill and experience of the hunter, more than the capricious fluctuations of chance. The availability of deer is fundamentally beyond the control of the hunter, in the hands of a power much less tangible.[64]

For the Saami, this means putting faith in some form of 'reindeer' being. The animals themselves are considered capable of speaking and reasoning, and most significantly at all, once hunted are thought to accept their fate, rather than having their lives taken from them. The implication of this belief is that, in order to avoid offending the reindeer spirit and thus losing access to the herd in future years, each animal must be treated with care and respect, and in particular hunting must be undertaken according to particular rules.[65] Moreover, the 'reindeer spirit' may be acknowledged, and tribute paid, through the maintenance of shrines. These shrines, often referred to as *sjeddes* or *siedde*, tend to be situated at topographically dramatic, often liminal locations in the landscape (such as caves, cliffs and waterside sites), and may be identified by the presence of 'sacrifices'. A number feature reindeer antlers on the outside, with collections of animal bones and food remains within. Such sacrifices seem to fulfil a range of roles: they request the continued availability of reindeer and other game, as well as protecting against ill weather, death and disease.[66]

Though perhaps at odds with the Christian world view, such a position would not have struck the Norse observer as particularly extraordinary. Nonetheless, descriptions of encounters with the Saami ('Lapps') in sagas and other documentary and literary sources are frequently expressed in terms of magic, even witchcraft. Though descriptions are not always pejorative (Saami elders are often thought of as wise, and are called upon to teach or counsel Germanic Scandinavians), there is a clear sense that they were seen as the Other.[67]

The explanation for this may perhaps lie in the Saami belief in animism and shamanic mysticism.[68] In this circumpolar world view, people and animals alike – as well as elements of the landscape in which they coexist – are seen as sentient, interconnected beings, often imbued with supernatural powers. The barriers that separate man and animal are seen as permeable, such that particular individuals – best known to us as shamans – are able to pass between worlds in a manner that is simply not deemed possible in the modern western cosmology. In the present context of course, the most significant facet of this world view relates to the human relationship with reindeer, but we should be careful not to reduce it to this; the Saami's perceptions of the world they inhabited would have influenced their relationships with all elements of the environment, and consequently had a tangible impact upon behaviour patterns and social organisation.

In terms of day-to-day activities, Viking-Age Saami populations would have been broken up into small bands, which, if not fully egalitarian, were at least characterised by limited specialisation in the roles played by individuals, other than that related to the sexes.[69] Nonetheless, we might identify 'task groups' formed around particular activities, such as hunting or fishing, and an overall flexible structure, with the possibility of frequent changes in leadership according to perceived ability, rather than personal wealth, strength or the exchange of gifts. The system was thus very different to that which operated in Norse society, and elsewhere in early medieval Europe, where power was vested in individuals, and was held largely according to military might, ability to inspire awe and loyalty through the giving of gifts, and, especially later on, through the holding of property.[70] However, the Saami system, with its inherent flexibility and lack of a formal hierarchy (at least one that we would easily recognise), represents a prudent adaptation to the problem of dependence upon a resource – the reindeer – whose location is subject to considerable movement.[71] In such a world, kinship would have been important, and many small bands would have been made up of families, or small groups of families.

These bands would congregate together in larger groups at certain times of the year, and disperse at others. In particular, we can expect that they separated into small groups (perhaps along familial lines) in the winter, in order to go about trapping animals for the fur trade, and then came together again in the summer for trade, fishing and to engage in the autumn reindeer hunt. They may thus have met at well-understood points in the landscape: trading posts, waterside sites and intercept points on the reindeer migration routes. Perhaps these meetings shared functions, so that the antler, meat and hides acquired in the autumn hunt were quickly traded on at these aggregations. In such a scenario, we need not envision carcasses, meat or secondary products being carried any great distance by the Saami themselves. This would have been a difficult proposition in the absence of large numbers of domestic reindeer that could be used as pack animals or to pull sleds. Instead, items were purchased by Scandinavians and other visitors to the market, and taken away using *their* means of transport. In this regard, it is interesting to think back to the Adamvalldá trail, which led from the water's edge up though the mountains of the Saami interior.

We should not necessarily think about such meetings as constituting anything like market exchange in the sense that we understand it; it is difficult to be sure whether items and materials were taxed or extorted from the Saami, or whether the latter stood to benefit from the exchange; in all likelihood the situation varied according to context.[72] However, we might suggest that the Saami did hold an important card, not only in having access to sought-after materials that were not widely available, but also in that they possessed the skills and experience necessary to collect them – a sort of technological capital.

The markets themselves were 'impermanent' and 'fluid'; parallels might be made with the African beach markets that later served medieval trade in the Indian Ocean. Such an arrangement was well suited to the Saami way of life. However, it is notable that the Viking Age seems to show evidence of a change in the structure and behaviour of Saami society, and there is much debate regarding the degree to which the appearance/expansion of an external market for northern materials influenced this change. In one view, hunting activity – presumably in reaction to the increased demand for furs of animals such as wolverine, rabbit and bear – seems to have encouraged a settlement expansion into the Norwegian–Swedish border area. Here, from the ninth century, we find the remains of (permanent or impermanent) buildings with sunken floors and surrounding walls of peat, particularly in areas either side of the edge of the taiga. The sites are distributed in small groups, lie close to trapping pits and have been widely interpreted as pre-pastoral dwellings; seasonal bases for small hunting parties.[73] Though some specialists argue that these settlements – often referred to as *stallo* sites – are related to a way of life that incorporates a pastoral element,[74] and others suggest that they relate to Norse–Saami integration under such an arrangement,[75] a more popular view is that they evidence the Saami response to the opportunities afforded by the fur trade, and their entrance on to the margins of the international stage as a result of this. The presence of exotic goods in Saami settlements is testament to their involvement with Norse communities in the south and, indirectly, even further afield. Northern products such as furs, skins, walrus ivory and sinew, were desirable prestige items for the elite of Viking-Age Europe, and some of these later became important commodities in commercial exchange;[76] reindeer pelts and antlers were no doubt similarly exported. Though these products are rarely enumerated in documentary sources, given that it was necessary to kill large numbers of animals for winter survival,[77] it would be natural to make use of the whole animal, including the antlers, and we know that there was certainly a market for the latter.

Provisioning the Combmaker

The next question is, of course, how the hunter passed on their raw antler to the combmaker. Was it exchanged as recovered, or processed first, so that bulky, low-utility sections (such as the burr) could be left behind, and the remainder cut into straighter, more easily transportable lengths? In certain times and places, it may not have been as complex as this. Prior to the Viking Age, for example, it has been suggested that mountain hunters and combmakers were one and the same. The case is not yet well proven, but there is an intriguing co-occurrence of putative hunting equipment and specialist tools in a number of furnished graves in alpine southern Norway.[78] More convincing is the presence of unfinished comb components in waste material from the late first/early second-millennial hunting site of Vesle Hjerkinn.[79] Assuming that such a practice did indeed take place, we might envision hunters trapping large numbers of reindeer in late autumn, at the time when both skins and antlers were in prime condition. The hunters then converted the raw antler into combs, either for trade at market, or to commission for aristocratic magnates. If this situation did indeed pertain, a number of questions remain to be asked: for whom were the combs being produced? How was exchange mediated, and transport facilitated? And, most intriguingly of all, to what community would such hunter-artisans have belonged – put simply, the Norse, or the Saami? At present it is difficult to be sure, but the answer is important; presumably this early model would have developed into the more structured system of production that characterised the Viking Age (see Chapter 3).

Modelling Antler Provision

Taking the above archaeological, ethnographic and – above all – ecological information into account, we are left with a choice. Two explanatory models are available to us. In the first, which we may call the *hunter-collector* model, a number of reindeer are trapped on their autumn migration, for their meat and pelts (which are, at this point in the year, in optimal condition; see above). A few months later, after the rut, bull reindeer begin to shed their antler, and these are systematically collected for use in combmaking and other crafts, or exchanged with artisans involved in such activities (as far as can be determined from inspection of waste material, supported by knowledge of the size and structure of reindeer antlers, we should assume that the key material required by combmakers was bull antler, rather than that of the cows). This model would work best if very large quantities of antler were required, as it is not dependent on the slaughter of large numbers of animals. However, it does seem to entail an extraordinary degree of endeavour, as it necessitates following the deer all the way to the site of the rut, and then waiting on their shedding, which may take some time.[80] Such an arrangement may explain the apparent dominance of shed antler amongst the large collections of reindeer waste from the combmaking workshops of the medieval Scandinavian towns. Output at these sites was on a scale greater than that seen in the Viking Age, and at Kungahälla (western Sweden), where combmakers appear to have used imported reindeer antler as their chief raw material, shed antler dominates.[81] The *hunter-collector* model thus works well in a scenario in which there is a need to secure a consistently high quantity of antlers year after year. Such a model is arguably less well suited to the smaller-scale production of the Viking Age.

A second possibility then, which we may call the *hunter* model, simply involves the autumn trapping of reindeer for both antler and skins, in numbers that would not destabilise the population. This seems to be the most efficient, and most likely model; indeed in the later medieval period, presumably in the quest for increased materials to support the combmaking industry, by now a large industry, these drives were expanded at places like Sumtangen, Hardangervidda, and escalated to such an extent that they began to seriously deplete populations. It is interesting, however, to note that this model is not well supported in the archaeological evidence (see below).

To summarise, we know that people have been hunting reindeer in Scandinavia as far back as the Ice Age, and the species has certainly been fundamental to the survival of hunter-gatherer populations for many millennia, providing food and clothing, as well as antler for working into tools. Indeed, the thick, warm, water-resistant, double-layered structure of reindeer hide has always made it perfect for the fabrication of cold-weather garments. Though much of the above is based upon ethnographic research, much of it nonetheless applies to our period of interest. As we have seen, it is in the years around the Viking Age that the evidence for hunting on a large scale starts to become apparent, and documentary sources from the medieval period allude to relationships with 'Lapps' (Saami), particularly regarding the goods that could be acquired from them (furs, ivories, and falcons) and their mystical powers. Such powers include, for example, the 'magical' properties of a reindeer cloak.[82] As we have seen, major archaeological studies have taken place in the Dovre and Hardangervidda areas; here and elsewhere in the mountains of central Norway we can identify extensive landscapes of hunting, pit traps, fences and bow rests.[83] While reindeer products are rarely explicitly mentioned in documentary or literary accounts, the significance of antler at least is clear, and the hunting landscapes attest to their being targeted; many of these traps are unnecessarily large for the chief quarry – rabbits, squirrels, wolverine or pine marten – and their sheer number is inconsistent with a function as bear traps. The connection between hunting and antler supply therefore seems clear.

From Hunting to Herding

This tradition, however, took a distinctive turn at some point between the Viking Age and the early modern period.[84] The human–reindeer relationship began to transform from one of hunter and prey to a much more interdependent arrangement of near-domestication. In this way of working, which allowed the herder to add milk, transport and draught power to the repertoire of resources already attainable through a close relationship with reindeer,[85] the animals were allowed to roam freely, but with the herders travelling with them on their annual migration.

It is worth noting that for some archaeologists,[86] the appearance of the *stallo* sites (see above) constitutes evidence for the dawn of reindeer pastoralism. In this reading, the sites are read as the seasonal settlements of migrating family groups of Saami, as they track the movements of the herd between taiga and mountain plateau. It is for this reason that some brief consideration of the pastoralist lifestyle is necessary, but it should be noted that this early date (600 years earlier than some estimates) is not widely accepted.[87]

Nonetheless, the possibility that an element of pastoral activity complemented a strategy dominated by reindeer-hunting cannot be dismissed out of hand. At the very least, a few reindeer must have been domesticated for use as decoys, draught or pack animals, and it is easy to see how this may have developed into exploitation for milk. Indeed, it is notable that Othere (a ninth-century Norwegian visitor to Wessex's royal court, and a key source for the description of northern Scandinavia) seems to have told King Alfred that he held 600 reindeer, but it is also clear from this and other accounts that the Saami ('Finnas') were known for their hunting way of life at this time. Perhaps the *Norse*, with Saami involvement, were herding reindeer in the Viking Age.[88] Furthermore, animal trapping was undoubtedly taking place on a large scale, but it has been argued that the main attraction of the reindeer hunt was meat, rather than hides, and perhaps we need to divorce the study of these two phenomena.

Whatever the detail, if reindeer pastoralism was being practised in Viking-Age Scandinavia, then we need to consider the way in which it may have operated, and any potential articulation with the supply of the craft of combmaking. You will recall that female reindeer produce milk between May and November, and this is key to the organisation of a pastoral economy. The milk is not produced in great quantity, but is nutritious, and ethnographic accounts demonstrate that pastoral societies were able to extract enough milk to see them through the summer, and to preserve further quantities as more long-lived dairy products for use in the cold winter months. The key development from hunting to pastoralism has been characterised as a reduction in herd movement, presumably brought about by the influence of breeding from domestic stock.[89] However, the need to stimulate the production of high-quality milk over a prolonged period nonetheless requires regularly moving the animals to new pastures though the milking season. In response to this, the herders (who move in relatively small family groups, without coming together into the large aggregations as are necessary for the reindeer hunt) seem to have developed a system whereby they cycle between a series of temporary camps, each separated from the next by a relatively short distance.[90]

Given that milk is only produced by adult female reindeer, a focus on dairy production inevitably has implications for the management of the herd at large. Today, reindeer-herding societies do not tend to slaughter young animals, although a few may be taken for their skins. Surplus males are rarely killed until late in life, but are frequently castrated (a task for many years undertaken with the teeth), while females are not slaughtered until after they have ceased to be fertile, if at all.[91] In such a situation, antlers must be collected from the ground, rather than through butchery. Such a scenario has implications for the acquisition of antler. Assuming that bull antler was the preferred source, the quantity of material available from culling would be relatively low, and castrated animals do appear to grow outwardly normal antlers, which could be harvested annually.[92] If reindeer antler was sourced from herding populations, then the collection of shed material would be the more practical solution. Indeed, it has the advantage over the use of butchered material in that the animals are not killed, and the resource is thus sustainable over the long term. The herd could thus (almost) be thought of as one might a flock of sheep kept for their wool. Depending on the chronology of pastoralisation (which, as we have seen, is a little fuzzy), it is even possible that the potential of a regular and sustainable annual supply of antler was one of a number of drivers behind the development of the reindeer pastoral economy. However, such speculations are, of course, simply that.

A good test of the likelihood of raw material being drawn from a pastoral or hunting economy would be to determine how much of the combmaking waste material in the late Viking-Age and medieval towns of Norway comprised shed antler, compared to butchered material. Such deposits have not yet been comprehensively studied with this question in mind, but where analyses have taken place, they do seem to be dominated by shed antler.[93] Superficially at least, this would seem at odds with a hunting economy, and may suggest that the bulk of the material was sourced through a pastoral system. However, this interpretation is based on counts of 'shed' and 'butchered' antler burrs (basal sections), which make up a relatively small proportion of the overall assemblage. Moreover, in the case of Norwegian material in particular, such a count may be biased by a sort of 'schlepp effect', wherein antler was processed down to transportable units prior to its being shipped out of the mountains. Such a process would inevitably lead to the under-representation of burrs, particularly of any that were still 'on the head'. These last might well have been simply chopped or sawn from the carcass, and if the cut was made through the beam itself, the diagnostic burr would be left attached to the cranium. As it stands, while I personally find the idea of material being sourced through hunters more attractive, there is too much room for doubt for any firm conclusions to be reached, and in the absence of compelling evidence in support of either model, the verdict must remain open.

Concluding Thoughts:
Deer and Humans in Viking-Age Landscapes

So far then, we've assessed the relationship between people, animals and landscape necessary in order to reliably supply the craft of combmaking.[94] The obvious next question relates to the identities of the collectors. Unfortunately, few of the collectors have left archaeological traces that allow them to be identified as such, and we have very little to tell us about their ethnicity, social standing, age or gender. Nonetheless, a few suggestions might be made.

Working with red deer, elk or reindeer are very different propositions, and to some extent these differences would lead to distinctive lifestyles. Perhaps, in areas of shared distribution, collectors engaged in the collection of antler from more than a single species, but from what we have seen so far, we can expect some degree of species-specialism. In southerly climes, where elk and red deer were the primary quarry, hunters may have played their part, but it may be better to imagine a role in primary collection or secondary accumulation for the wardens of noble estates. In northern Scandinavia, in contrast, our collectors may have been Norse or Saami, hunters, trappers or pastoralists.

Graves in Norway suggest that these hunters may also have been combmakers, but as we have seen, such an arrangement does not necessarily mean that they acquired the entirety of their antler from butchered animals. Hunters understand the lie of the land, climate and weather, and animal behaviour, so would be perfectly situated to exploit the range of natural resources they encountered. Thus, the act of tracking for hunting may have led them to the sites of shed antlers; there is considerable overlap in the skills and observations necessary in hunting and tracking, after all. Moreover, combining these tasks may have allowed the practitioner to be gainfully occupied for longer periods of the year, while the activities themselves could easily be seen as mutually supportive; tracking could be undertaken in the winter, ahead of hunting, in order to identify hunting grounds for the following season, and sourcing shed antlers would assist in this process while simultaneously constituting a useful resource in themselves. Contemporary collectors in the US frequently hunt too, but take time out for collection in late winter. Our hunters may have gone on specialised collection expeditions, just as today's hunters do, and may even have used the exercise as an initiation for apprentices, much as is done today.[95] The collection of antler can thus be seen as skilled practice, as something of a technology in itself. Moreover, if we choose to believe that a number of these hunters and gatherers of antler were also combmakers, then such a shared occupation would suggest a depth of understanding of source and material throughout the process from recovery to manufacture. Such a scenario would have implications for the manner in which manufacture was undertaken; what has been called, in other contexts, 'truth to material'.[96] This is an exciting proposition: that the connections between landscape, animal and material were not lost upon collection, but were rather preserved intact even to the point of manufacture. We might thus imagine the combmaker remembering the collection of a particular antler, placing it in his mind in relation to topography, to past events, even to particular animals. Perhaps on occasion such narratives were communicated to the purchasers of combs, such that they were aware of their comb's early biography, and could tie it to particular (perhaps exotic) parts of the landscape.

Who knows? For now, these ideas are raised simply as possibilities. As it stands, we have amassed a collection of antler as raw material, but have not yet fashioned it into combs. This is the task of Chapter 3.

3

Ways of Working,
Ways of Making

*Three things that constitute a comb-maker: racing a hound in contending
for a bone; straightening a ram's horn by his breath, without fire; chanting
upon a dunghill so that all antlers and bones and horns that are below
come to the top*

Triads of Ireland, 117[1]

We have seen the efforts and logistics involved in the sourcing of raw
materials for combmaking. This, combined with the complexities of
manufacture itself (discussed below), might lead us to question why
anyone would even bother. It is thus worth considering how combmaking
came about, the way in which it developed and the reasons it did so.

If we trace the sequence back to its absolute genesis, we come to the
question of why humans ever make objects.[2] At their root, tools make
tasks – and life – easier, but they also open up new opportunities. Past
generations of archaeologists and anthropologists have divided the
manufactured world into objects that are purely functional, and those
that are in some way invested with special properties, whether they be
aesthetic, magical, symbolic or in some other way meaningful; a stone axe
might be an example of the former category, an ivory pendant of the latter.
But of course things are not so easily classified. Axes have been shown
to have considerable meaningful content,[3] while roles given to amulets
and pendants that might to us seem rather 'magical' or 'supernatural' may
be seen by their users in purely functional terms. And the comb provides
a good example of an artefact that, on first analysis, appears to have a
pretty straightforward job to do (cleaning and dressing hair), but, when
considered further, carries out a wide range of social and economic roles
(see Chapters 4 and 5).

Let's go back then, to the first imagining of a comb. In early prehistory, our hominin ancestors would of course have paid attention to their hair, through personal and mutual grooming; we see this in the behaviour of apes today.[4] That first leap, to the production of a tool that groomed the hair more efficiently than did the hand, was a simple, yet most important step. That first comb may have been simply a handful of sticks or rushes, but it wouldn't have taken long before it was realised that something more sturdy and reliable was required, something that could be used again and again. Given the difficulty of working wood so finely (with flint tools), eventually bone would have been identified as an appropriate medium for such a venture. This material would have been a visible and recognised medium in hunter-gatherer communities, and it has been shown that early human societies were experimenting to great effect with the physical and aesthetic qualities of bone, shell, and ivory.[5] Moreover, there is already evidence of the powerful hold that the deer had on the imaginations of Palaeolithic and Mesolithic communities,[6] and antler may have already started to recommend itself for both its physical and symbolic attributes (which, as we have seen, may have in fact been indivisible).

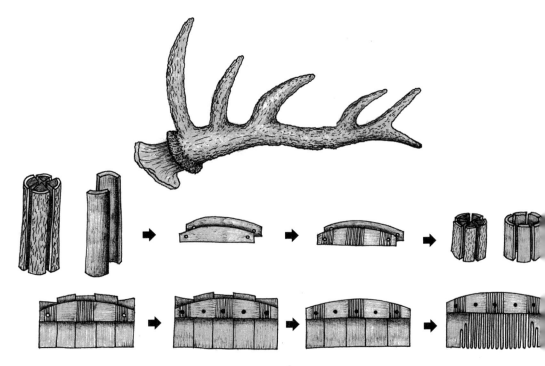

5. A schematic representation of the standard manufacturing process. (Drawing by Hayley Saul)

Once the material was set, the development of the comb began apace. Metal combs are known from later prehistoric contexts,[7] but these would no doubt have been the preserve of the elite, and bone and antler seem to have remained the more accessible medium for comb manufacture. Pre-Roman Iron-Age examples were made on the longbones of mammals, and by this point we know that the dressing of hair was important; the bog bodies of northern Europe testify to a diversity and complexity of styles. And it wasn't long before the next great leap was made: the production of complex combs comprising numerous individually manufactured elements.

Composite comb manufacture seems to have had its origins in the 'Germanic' parts of northern Europe, and the fundamentals of the process seem to have crystallised by the end of the Roman period, such that a similar sequence of manufacture was undertaken by the combmaker in late Roman, Anglo-Saxon, Viking-Age and medieval society. It is thus worth outlining this process in a little detail (see fig. 5).

How to Make a Good Comb

The artisan takes a good, solid section of antler tine from his cache of pre-cut lengths of material. The piece feels heavy, its surface is hard and rough, and there is a nice, thick layer of dense, bony material outside the spongy core. It feels right; this is the good antler. Using a hammer, and a wedge itself made of the tip of an antler tine, the combmaker splits the section down its length, first in half, then into quarters. He then clamps each piece in turn and, taking a rasp or chisel, quickly scrapes away the soft, porous material from the antler's underside. He then turns it over, and similarly removes its rough, hard outer surface, thus revealing a number of solid, compact, eminently useable lengths of antler. These are further filed down to form pieces of roughly plano-convex section, before they are bound together in pairs, and shaped into matching sets of gently bowed plates. These will be the connecting plates of the comb: the components that not only bind the comb together, but also act as both handhold and field for decoration. Indeed, the combmaker may have chosen to decorate the plates at this stage, carefully marking out vertical or horizontal lines, cross-hatching or interlace, before incising them with a simple scribing tool. More complex designs, such as chains of 'ring and dot' ornament, could be applied using a range of specialised scribing tools, and no little skill.

Once the connecting plates have been dealt with, the combmaker may move on to the creation of toothplates. These are produced by quartering short, cylindrical sections of beam, just as was done in the production of connecting plates, before finishing them to thin, flat, rectangular billets. Once the combmaker has prepared a pair of connecting plates, and four or more toothplate billets (depending on the length of the intended comb), he may begin to assemble the comb itself. The billet array is lined up between the two connecting plates and, following a certain amount of adjustment for regularity and evenness, the comb is permanently fixed together. A simple hand drill would have been used to make a number of perforations along the length of the comb, carefully positioned with both comb strength and overall aesthetics in mind. The holes would then have been fixed with bone, bronze or, most commonly, iron rivets. These would have been acquired from a smith, and experiment has shown that they could be inserted cold, by gentle peening into the holes. Ornament may have been applied at this stage, just prior to the drilling of rivet holes, or later in the sequence. Detailed recording of the relationship between rivets and decoration allows archaeologists to determine the likely order in which this took place for any given comb.

Either way, attention is paid to aesthetics at this point, as the upper edges of the toothplates, extending above the back of the connecting plates, are trimmed back using a saw, and decorative profiling may be added to endplates. The object now looks very much like a comb, but for the fact that it is non-functional. The next task is thus to cut and shape the teeth. With the comb clamped firmly in place, a fine-bladed saw, much like a modern hacksaw or coping saw, is used to carefully cut the teeth. These are frequently so fine and even that some have suggested a double-bladed saw may have been used, though no such tool has been found from Viking levels. However it was done, this was a job for a steady and experienced hand, as the whole comb could be ruined at this stage.[8] Once they had been cut, the teeth were then carefully sharpened to a point and shaped along their length, in order to maximise functional effectiveness, as well as for aesthetic appearance. Aesthetics then come to the fore, as the comb is burnished or polished with a coarse-grained material such as sharkskin or pumice, while pigments and colouring agents may also have been employed in order to highlight incised decoration.

Archaeological evidence – in the form of tools, manufacturing waste and the finished objects themselves – show us that this was the way in which the majority of combs were manufactured. But that is not to say that there was no room for choice in the process; the combs were produced by people, not machines. Different tools and techniques could be used, and though the rationale for making a particular manufacturing decision may often have been unspoken, the study of such technological choices has much archaeological potential. This is the subject of our next discussion.

Ideas and Innovations:
The Archaeology of Technological Choice

What governs the decisions made by an artisan in manufacturing an object? The choices made may very often be unconscious or taken for granted, but they remain central to the character of production, and ultimately of the object itself. For an understanding of this phenomenon, we must turn to anthropology.

It has been shown that the techniques used in making an object are invariably *learned* behaviours.[9] The manner in which a particular task is undertaken is contingent upon social context; a comb may thus be made in subtly different ways in Viking-Age England, Norway or Russia. These different 'ways of making' develop out of local or regional traditions; like Newton's First Law, once a good way to manufacture a comb has been found, it will take some considerable external impulse to convince the craftsperson to adopt a new approach. Given that different ways of undertaking the same task might develop in different situations, the driver behind technological choice cannot simply be efficiency, but rather social circumstance. Historians of modern technology and science are well aware of this; the trajectory of innovation, from idea to finished product, is not some pure, straightforward sequence of innovation, demonstration of fitness for purpose and adoption, but rather a more messy network of decisions, biases and accidents, subject to the actions of powerful individuals and interest groups.[10] Though the Viking world was very different to our own, the basic concept – that technologies develop out of social context – remains valid.

Of course, the materials being worked place certain constraints upon the artisan – it is impossible to make a comb from leather, for instance – but they do far more than this. Indeed, to the experienced artisan, the properties of a material present themselves as opportunities, they supply the potential for making particular objects in particular ways.[11] Moreover, the key properties of a material are not limited to physical attributes, but may include cultural and symbolic qualities, superstitions or beliefs about the proper ways in which to deal with a given material, and unspoken rules about the ways in which certain objects should be made.[12] Once we accept this, it is easy to see how manufacturing methods might vary across diverse social and political environments. To the artisans themselves, choices may not even be being made, such is the degree to which ways of making are rooted in experience, inherited knowledge and tradition. Thus, crafters working in different times or places may well argue that their way of making an object is the best, or even the *only* way to do it, but others working elsewhere would disagree.

These ideas obviously throw a questioning light on the validity of the standard sequence of comb manufacture discussed above. Of course, to a considerable degree combmaking *was* a standardised process, and in some elements of the process the degree of convergence between the techniques applied in Scandinavia and the British Isles are startling; there seem to be common 'ideal' tooth gauges, as well as consistencies in toothplate widths and thicknesses, and these are independent of material used. Nonetheless, within the process there is space for variability. On a very basic level, antler may have been acquired intact, or in measured lengths, whereupon it may have been treated (through soaking in water or solutions containing milk or vegetable matter, for instance) or untreated.[13] Different tools (saws or wedges, files or rasps, clamps or vices) may have been used. Diverse rivet materials could be used (iron, bone and both pegs and rolled sheets of copper alloy are known), and there are a range of ways in which rivets could be fixed (fig. 6). Similarly, ornament offers considerable potential for

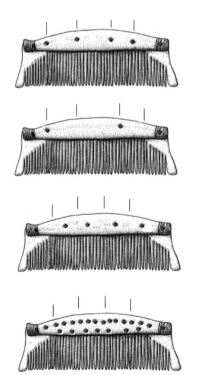

artistic choice, and might thus be applied in diverse ways, and at different stages in the sequence.[14] Even the finishing of a comb may have varied – was this comb to be highly polished or coloured? How would its teeth be shaped? More significantly, to some combmakers the manufacture of a comb may have been conceptualised as a coherent process, such that the comb was in some sense 'chiselled' out of a single antler,[15] while to others production would have been serialised, with large numbers of blanks being stockpiled for use at a later date. Such different modes of production would of course develop out of different organising structures, working environments and

6. Various techniques used in the riveting of combs. Vertical lines represent toothplate edges. (Drawing by Sven Schroeder and Steve Ashby)

economies, and no doubt varied in both time and space. Ways of working would have been passed on from generation to generation; apprentices would slowly learn to develop the correct techniques for making a comb, as they listened, observed and accumulated experience with tools and materials. Thus, variations might be apparent on a regional canvas, but we can expect some degree of consistency and conservatism over time, as generations of combmakers continued to manufacture according to the tenets and rules with which they were familiar and comfortable.

When we take the time to look for them, these variations are apparent, for all that the combs tend to look the same on a superficial level. Chronological change is slow and episodic, and tends to be visible in overall morphology, rather than in manufacturing techniques. Thus, there is a tangible shift in the size, form and ornament of combs popular through the period between the ninth and eleventh centuries, and we might explain this in terms of a transition from a world in which combs were manufactured as individual commissions for elite magnates, to one in which they were produced on a large scale for an expanding commercial market (see below). As for spatial patterning, different parts of Scandinavia, the British Isles, and continental Europe all have readily apparent traditions in terms of riveting technique, and different defaults when it comes to raw material (governed to some degree, though not entirely, by local availability). Thus, the combs produced in the Anglo-Scandinavian towns of York and Lincoln were made in subtly different ways to those from Scandinavia and on the continent.[16] Though doubtless inspired by Scandinavian templates, both raw materials and manufacturing techniques were distinctive. That said, combs within England do seem to share common traits; we may even speak of an English school of manufacture. If English combmakers were to have come into contact with their Scandinavian counterparts (or their products), we might expect them to have noted the differences in manufacturing techniques. It is difficult to say whether they would have adopted elements of their technique, or looked upon them disparagingly, but it is notable that Scandinavian and English modes of comb manufacture (and riveting in particular) persist along different trajectories throughout the Viking and medieval periods.[17] Of course, the failure to adopt one another's approaches does not necessarily imply a lack of contact, and may equally relate to an active rejection of alien ways of making. The adoption or otherwise of innovations is always contingent upon a range of social and economic factors.[18] One key factor would have been the manufacturer's lifestyle, to which we now turn.

Modelling Movement and Manufacture

So far, we have introduced the basic sequence of actions that may lead to the production of a comb, and we have briefly discussed the degree to which this sequence might be mutable, subject to adaptation contingent upon social environment. However, if the world in which an artisan worked was so fundamental to the way in which they produced their goods, it is incumbent upon us to spend a little time thinking *about* that world. How were the combmaker's life and work structured? Where did they work? With whom did they come into contact? These are the issues we need to address. In so doing, we will not only be able to make more sense of comb manufacture and trade, but will also illuminate the social world of the Viking Age more generally.

Craft and industry have long been subjects of interest to archaeologists, and as a result, early medieval combmaking has seen considerable attention over the last forty years or so.[19] Many scholars have been concerned with scale of manufacture, and having identified the distinctive debris associated with the production sequence outlined above, have noted what they perceive to be the small size of such waste deposits. Though this phenomenon was initially explained as the result of combmakers working on a part-time basis, or producing a range of objects in different materials (such as amber, for instance),[20] it is now more generally seen as evidence of combmakers living an itinerant lifestyle.[21] That is to say that they travelled around from market to market, working in rented workshops, taking advantage of the economic potential provided by the large gatherings of people that occurred on a regular basis in the towns, trading centres, beach and lake markets of the Viking world.

There is much to recommend this model. For one thing, it explains how a combmaker could make a living from the production of an object that appears, on the face of it, to have been in limited demand (one may presume that few people would have had more than one comb, and would only need a replacement when one was broken or lost). By moving around, and focusing on large gatherings, the combmaker always had a market for their product.

However, there are problems with the argument, on both logical and evidential grounds. The travelling artisan would need to have a ready supply of raw materials; carrying them from place to place would be uneconomical to say the least, while to rely on their availability when one got to market would seem to be logistically difficult, and would make the combmaker vulnerable to exploitation at the hands of the dealer.

There is also a lack of clarity in this model; what does 'itinerancy' really mean? For instance, on what scale did these artisans move? It is perfectly feasible, for instance, that combmaking in northern England was characterised by a well-trodden mercantile circuit that saw combmakers travelling between markets at towns such as York and Lincoln. In northern Europe, the Baltic Sea provides an ideal medium for rapid transit between the markets and urban centres at Kaupang (Norway), Ribe (Denmark), Birka (central Sweden), Hedeby (northern Germany) and Wolin (northern Poland) and it is conceivable that combmakers and other artisans travelled on just such a circuit.[22] As well-practised as early medieval society was in maritime navigation, however, it seems unlikely that combmakers would have relied on far-distant markets, and trans-North Sea travel cannot have made up a frequent part of the combmaker's cycle of activities.

Quite apart from the question of scale of operation, ambiguity remains regarding the regularity or persistence with which an itinerant artisan might find themselves travelling. For instance, did these combmakers have a homebase? May they have made their products at home, and travelled primarily as merchants, simply adding piecemeal to their stock as they went? Such nuances have rarely been considered in the debate, but they are key if such a model is to be accepted.[23] In later contexts, documentary evidence tells us that combmakers operated out of rural workshops, and simply brought their wares to larger urban centres for trade on market days, though of course the environment within which these nineteenth-century craftspeople worked was very different to that experienced by our Viking-Age combmakers.[24] There is of course space for regional variability in organisation. There is no reason to assume that combmakers would have worked in the same way, at all times, in all places. Rather, local and regional differences in politics, economics, competition, available resources, and urban environments would surely have made all the difference to how a combmaker maximised the use of their time.

Turning to the evidential bases, the 'itinerancy' model is founded primarily on the small size of waste deposits at places like Hedeby, Birka, and Ribe (fig. 7), and a perceived lack of variation in comb form and ornament across Europe. However, one of the fundamental tenets of archaeological interpretations is that absence of evidence does *not* equal evidence of absence. That is to say that the archaeological record is by its very nature fragmentary, so that a failure to find evidence of a structure or activity at a site should not be uncritically interpreted as proof that that phenomenon did not exist. What little we understand of the process of taphonomy (everything mechanical, physical, chemical and biological that happens to archaeological material from the moment of its deposition) demands that we avoid such simplistic equations. This idea has particular implications for the quantification of combmaking debris;

it is a mistake to assume that that small size of waste deposits has any direct or identifiable relationship to the number of products produced on site, or to the length of time for which the activity was undertaken. In many cases, only small areas of settlement sites have been excavated to date, so any extrapolation as to the scale or organisation of industry must necessarily be tentative. Moreover, why would we expect artisans to work up to their knees in waste material, or even assume that all their rubbish was dumped in their backyards? In this regard, it is notable that many of northern Europe's key comb-producing sites (e.g. those at York, Ribe, Hedeby and Birka) are situated close to waterfronts or harbours, and the degree to which medieval industries exploited rivers and waterways for waste disposal is well known.[25] In short, the argument that small waste deposits relate to short-term activity is – while superficially appealing – unproven.[26]

The second string to the 'itinerancy' bow is the perceived formal and ornamental similarity of European combs. This is explained through the idea that travelling combmakers regularly met one another on the market circuit – perhaps they even travelled together as part of an itinerant community of artisans – and thus exchanged ideas, templates, and innovations, ultimately resulting in a uniform corpus.[27] This to my mind sounds like special pleading, and a case could equally be made for itinerancy leading to a lack of uniformity. But this is beside the point, as the supposed uniformity of Viking combs is in fact an illusion. There is a

similarity in the early Viking Age, but while the combs around the Baltic region may perhaps have been produced and distributed by a ring of travelling craftspeople, it is unrealistic to attempt to tie the British Isles into this circuit. It is far more likely that these combs reached England, Scotland and Ireland in the hands of raiders and settlers, with the possible addition of a number of diplomatic gifts (this explanation may even apply equally to the Baltic). By the tenth and eleventh centuries, regional

7. Combmaking debris from Hungate, York. (Image courtesy York Archaeological Trust)

styles are much more visible, and it is clear that the people manufacturing combs in Birka and Trondheim are certainly not the people making them in York and Southampton.

One perhaps stronger piece of evidence in favour of combmakers working on an itinerant basis is the presence of quantities of manufacturing waste at a number of coastal market sites in southern Scandinavia.[28] These sites were surely frequented by local populations, and served by travelling merchants, and if combmakers were not part of this latter community, then we have to explain their presence at these sites. It is of course possible that our artisans represented a local element within the market community, exploiting the opportunities provided by visits from merchant vessels, but the alternative – that they were themselves part of the travelling merchants' caravan – is perhaps the more parsimonious explanation. Nonetheless, the absence of sites of this character in the British Isles is notable; another reminder that we need not invoke the same mercantile system in diverse contexts.

In sum then, the British Isles are not easily incorporated into the model of northern European itinerant trade that has been widely adopted. I should note that we should not see the North Sea as a barrier; from a certain perspective it was quite the opposite, something of a medium for contact and communication.[29] However, this does not mean we have to accept that the craft and trade of combmaking was organised in the same way on all of its shores, or that it was dependent upon the actions and movement of a small number of very cosmopolitan artisans. Rather, I believe that combmaking took place in many different social, economic, political and environmental contexts, and that this regional variability is important.

What is more, the artefactual evidence for itinerancy – a perceived aesthetic uniformity – may be little more than mirage. The comb forms available to an Anglo-Saxon, pre-Viking consumer were diverse, and while there is greater uniformity in the 'type fossil' combs of the early Viking Age, this may be best explained in terms of a widespread distribution of combs from a limited 'home area'; that is, as a result of the ninth-century expansion out of Scandinavia that is often referred to as the Viking diaspora.[30] There is little to suggest that such combs were being manufactured in England or Scotland, where it is likely that 'pre-Viking' forms persisted for at least a time. By the tenth and eleventh centuries, Scandinavian settlement in the British Isles was much better established, and it is therefore no surprise to see combs being made in England according to Scandinavian style, but the methods by which they were produced were nonetheless distinctive, and are suggestive of either a sedentary, or *locally* itinerant mode of production. Again, it seems that manufacturing was undertaken according to regional traditions – traditions that had once shared a common origin but which had since diverged into particular, localised ways of making. Through travel, trade and contact with foreign merchants and artisans, combmakers working within these different 'schools' were no doubt aware of the fashions and forms being made and used elsewhere, but when it came to manufacturing methods, they stuck with their own tried and trusted techniques.

Community in Combmaking

In closing, it is important that we remember that our focus here is not the comb itself, not its method of production, not even the system within which its manufacturers operated, but rather the people that interacted with it throughout its life. Given that our concern in this chapter is manufacture, our gaze should shift to the combmakers themselves; are we able to shine a light on their lives in any meaningful way? Well, so far we have said a little about the experience of their everyday tasks, their feel for material and approaches to manufacture, and their likely degree of sedentism. But can we be more direct than that? What was it like to *be* a Viking-Age combmaker?

One way in which we may attempt to address such nebulous questions is through considering other peoples' perceptions of the combmaker. How were they perceived by their contemporaries: the potter, the farmer, the soldier, the beggar, the priest? It is a little unclear whether Viking-Age combmakers should be seen in the realm of talented, even supernaturally gifted craftspeople such as smiths,[31] or whether they were looked down upon as were their post-medieval successors.[32] Documentary references – such as the quote from the *Triads of Ireland* used at the head of this chapter – are ambiguous.

No doubt, of course, the combmaker's status varied with temporal context. In the pre-Viking period, a number could perhaps be described as 'master craftsmen', and such highly skilled artisans may have worked for local potentates on a permanent or *ad hoc* basis. However, by the Viking Age, the demand for highly skilled craftsmen in a competitive market may have been such that the combmaker enjoyed a status of some privilege. Nonetheless, in some situations we may need to envision combmakers as highly skilled slaves.[33]

By the middle of the Viking Age, though there is some degree of individual variation in comb form and ornament at sites such as Birka, in general terms the material from northern England and Atlantic Scotland is produced in greater numbers, and to a lower standard. The combmaker was probably no longer a master craftsperson (nor a slave), but rather a relatively independent artisan-merchant. Though their products seem to have been relatively inexpensive and easily accessible in the market from this point on, the continuing demand for combs surely says something positive about the combmaker's place in the social hierarchy of tenth- and eleventh-century Europe.

But there was more to the combmaker's identity than a simple hierarchical position. Identities may incorporate ethnicity, age, gender, regional upbringing, or, of course, profession. Might we conceive of some form of solidarity amongst combmakers? We might suggest that regional (or travelling) schools of manufacture gave rise to something of a mercantile identity. It is not unreasonable to suggest that the way in which these artisans worked may have had an impact upon the ways in which they were perceived in local communities. Whether the combmaker was a sedentary, fixed presence in the town, or an occasional (and perhaps even hotly anticipated) visitor to the marketplace would influence their place in the community. No doubt it would also colour their relationships with fellow artisans and merchants, including other combmakers. How closely were they able to work with the butcher, the metal-caster, the smith or the tanner? Did they see other combmakers as uninvited competition, or as welcome travelling companions? Of course, we may never know, but the detailed analyses of objects, manufacturing waste, and settlement sites of the kind discussed above constitute the best chance we have of getting at such questions. Technological choices and *ways of making* subtly acted to bind together communities of combmakers both in space (whether sedentary or itinerant) and in time (as apprenticeship allowed traditions to be passed on from generation to generation). Similar shared understandings of ways of living and acting would have held together communities on a range of scales, and in Chapter 5 we will look at a few aspects of such behaviour – those related to the display and use of hair combs. First, though, we need to take a step back, and consider why combmakers even existed, and why the comb became so important to the people of Viking-Age Europe. What was it about hair that necessitated this attention, this performance, even this obsession?

4

Technologies of Transformation

Every day they must wash their faces and heads and this they do in the dirtiest and filthiest fashion possible to wit, every morning a girl servant brings a great basin of water; she offers this to her master and he washes his hands and face and his hair – he washes it and combs it out with a comb in the water; then he blows his nose and spits into the basin. When he has finished, the servant carries the basin to the next person, who does likewise. She carries the basin thus to all the household in turn, and each blows his nose, spits, and washes his face and hair in it.

Ibn Fadlan, verse 84[1]

Consider the luxurious dress, hair and behaviour of leaders and people. See how you have wanted to copy the pagan way of cutting hair and beards. Are not these the people whose terror threatens us, yet you want to copy their hair?

Alcuin's letter to Aethelred, 131[2]

When I was a teenager, I had long hair. Long, curly hair that was impossible to control. And that was the point; I was making a conscious effort not to care for my hair, not to see it as in any way external to myself. But in hindsight of course, long, unkempt hair was a key component of the symbolic repertoire of the 'alternative' culture of the early 1990s. My decision not to pay attention to my hair was every bit as telling as would be the decision to style it every day. Long hair might not be a prescribed part of uniform in the same way as monastic tonsure or the military buzz cut, but this is simply a matter of degree, they are not *qualitatively* different. As a mutable, changing part of the body, and one that is both clearly visible and easily manipulable, hair is uniquely placed for the display of personal identity and status, the construction of boundaries, and the communication of social cues.

And so it always has been. Hair types and hair behaviours have long been in use as literary tropes, referring to age, gender, wisdom, honour, fertility and power. Of particular interest here is a story from the *Heimskringla*, a twelfth to thirteenth-century collection of sagas relating the histories of the kings of Norway. The *Heimskringla* relates that a ninth-century king named Harald, later to become Harald I, vowed never to 'cut nor comb his hair' until he had united Norway under his rule. He thus became known as Harald *Lufa* (Tanglehair), until his ultimate success a decade later, whereupon he took up the epithet *Hárfagri* ('Finehair' or 'Fairhair'). Of course, this story should not be taken at face value, but its use as a literary device clearly suggests that the reference – the importance of hair behaviour in the maintenance of elite identity – was at least understood by a medieval Nordic audience. It is also telling that this resonance is still understood today; though there is of course no implication of continuity, it is interesting to note that in 2010, the rapper 50 Cent made an oath (via the medium of Twitter, rather than saga) not to cut his hair until he had completed the production of his new record.

If we are to begin to understand the social role played by Viking-Age combs, and the amount of time, expertise and resources invested in their production, it is important to appreciate the social significance of hair and its maintenance in the Viking Age. This is the subject of the next two chapters. We will first explore the evidence – archaeological, literary, historical and iconographic – for attitudes to hair, and the ways in which it was used in display and communication, before moving on to discuss the means by which it was cared for, maintained and manipulated, and the contexts in which this happened. In an attempt to explain this peculiar, if generally unremarked-upon, preoccupation, we will turn to historical, ethnographic, anthropological and sociological studies of hair behaviour, and finally we will explore how all of this impacts upon the life of the key piece of kit in hair maintenance – the comb – and whether the object in itself became invested with the significance of its actions. In so doing, we'll learn about far more than just combs and hair; we'll have a window into the everyday lives of the Viking Age.

Writing Histories of Hair

If you've got this far into the book, I can probably assume that you're willing to believe that in the Viking Age, hair and its grooming were of some importance. But in what way were they socially or culturally significant? To answer such questions, archaeology needs a little help from its sister disciplines, and it might be possible to access some of this meaning through an approach that integrates archaeological, documentary and ethnographic evidence.

However, it will not do to simply propose an all-embracing significance of combs and hair. It would be short-sighted to assume that cultural or symbolic meaning is simply self-generating; the question is whether unique cultural relevances existed in particular regions, and how these were interconnected. For example, was there a particular Anglo-Scandinavian perception of hair, and if so, did this stem from Anglo-Saxon, Scandinavian, or other continental sources? Alternatively, was it created through the interaction of the current natives of Britain with Scandinavian settlers? Could the pan-European contacts that were opening up during this period also have had an influence? If we are to address these issues, we need to consider relevant sources not just from the Viking Age itself, but also from the preceding centuries in Britain, Scandinavia and other parts of western Europe. By this means, we may note similarities and differences in belief systems and social structures.

We can learn even more by extending our field of vision beyond historical societies. Considerable success in the conceptualisation of ritual, social and symbolic practice has been achieved through the application of ethnography (attempting to understand the context of particular practices through field observation). From observing present-day, non-western societies, explanations for otherwise uninterpretable patterns in archaeological data often present themselves. Given the lack of detailed written accounts of the ritual importance of hair and hairdressing in the Viking Age, the use of such analogies is fundamental to progress in understanding. Nonetheless, we need to take care in such approaches, as the perils of too broad-brush an application are clear and well documented.[3]

Explaining Hair Behaviour

In what follows, we will explore such anthropological theory in an attempt to consider the ways in which people may have thought about hair in the Viking Age. We will also look at iconography and literature from a range of contexts, to see how attitudes to hair – as represented in art – have varied in space and time. Over the course of the next few pages, I hope to show that in many contexts – including the Viking Age – hair may have had significance in relation to: identity and the structuring of society (along lines of status, ethnicity, group membership, age, gender, sexuality, and religion); personhood (an extension of the self); beauty, virtue and morality; and life, vitality, power, and magic. We will explore these phenomena using a variety of documentary, iconographic and archaeological sources. First though, it is necessary to briefly recount what we know about hair treatment in non-western societies.

Hair and Anthropology

In *The Golden Bough*, that classic of early anthropology, Sir James Frazer,[4] suggests that many disparate cultures pay special attention to hair, its cutting and grooming, because they believe that spirits exist within the hair and the head. The breadth of Frazer's study is phenomenal, but it is characterised by the rather eclectic approach typical of its time, such that its generalising statements do not really take us forward, and we will not dwell on it here. Instead, we pick up in the psychological and social anthropology of the 1950s, and in particular, the work of Charles Berg and Edmund Leach.

For Berg,[5] hair was almost universally a symbol of the genitals, and the growth of long hair represented an acceptance of the existence of sex, while shaving and haircutting could be seen as symbolised castration, something of an attempt to control primitive aggression and sexuality. However, Berg's beliefs were based on a somewhat uncritical application of Freudian theory (our attitudes to hair being founded in the genital and anal stages of development), and supported almost entirely by anecdotal evidence. Moreover, as Berg considered all 'hair behaviour' to stem from our unconscious (more specifically the conflict between id and superego), then his ideas find little utility in an archaeological sense, unless we are interested in the application of broad generalisations and covering laws.

Although critical of Berg's methods, Edmund Leach produced a collection of examples that broadly supported this hypothesis, suggesting that different attitudes to hair represent behavioural ideals.[6] Leach's case studies were compiled from a variety of anthropological sources, and cover media ranging from Shakespearean jokes to Buddhist imagery. Probably the most obvious example of haircutting as sexual ritual is tonsuring, ostensibly a symbol of the monk's celibacy. However, Leach provides further examples, relating mourning rituals and sexual abstinence with head-shaving. Indeed, this pattern finds numerous examples through history. Long hair is frequently taken to stand for unrestrained sexuality, short or bound hair as representative of those restricted in sexual freedom, and the shaven head as indicative of abstinence. A particularly celebrated example is the oft-cited English Civil War dichotomy of the royalist 'Cavaliers' (conventionally pictured as wearing their hair long, and caricatured as standing for a sort of easy-going freedom) and the puritanical 'Roundheads' (with their short-cropped hair and beliefs in restraint and austerity). To push the issue further, the act of dressing hair (as distinct from its growth or removal) may also have sexual significance. Leach demonstrates that while hairdressing may be connected to celibacy in Buddhist monastic institutions, it has other sexual connotations in the secular world, where it may be associated with pregnancy, parturition, clitidorectomy and homosexuality.

This may sound a little alien, and there are of course other interpretations, in which hair is less directly associated with sexuality. Could the monk's tonsure not be seen rather as a sign of monastic obedience or humility? Decades after Berg and Leach, it was argued that the growth or cutting of hair was closely related to the concept of social belonging.[7] Thus, short or shaven hair might suggest membership of society, while longer hair was indicative of some level of rejection of social norms. The evidence for this argument was drawn from classical and biblical references (see, for example, the case of lepers), while twentieth-century examples included an implicit opposition of the monk, soldier and convict against the 'intellectual', 'hippy' and 'woman'. Looking across time, we may identify a number of moments in time at which particular standards of 'hair behaviour' were seen as appropriate for certain social subgroups. For instance, in the New Testament, Paul's letters to the Corinthians seem to indicate that it was considered indecent for a woman of the early first millennial Mediterranean region to let her hair hang loose, and that this would shame her husband.[8] Moreover, the requirements for head covering during prayer were very different for men and women; it appears that there was a concern that women should keep their hair tied and covered, while men should not wear head covering of any kind. It has been suggested that the justification for this was the denial of sexuality, and a sign of submissiveness.[9]

These ideas clearly have at root some belief in the head and hair having a particular spiritual significance relative to other parts of the body. Indeed, head hair is frequently said to be the seat of the soul, and of course the residue of such belief is preserved in the Christian rituals of baptism and blessing.[10] Conversely, Sikhism sees unshorn hair as a sign of holiness, and its cutting is one of the four Kurehats (taboos).[11] In more secular circles, the head and hair are often seen to be related to power, and it is significant that the key symbol of royal office in western societies is the crown, and that the monarch's hair is anointed with oil upon coronation.[12] In all likelihood, such phenomena are in some way connected to their aforementioned religious corollaries.[13] It is thus rather difficult to unpick the spiritual, sexual and moral associations that combine to justify the use of hair as a signifier of social inclusion or exclusion.

Notwithstanding any postmodern doubts about such pigeonholing, there is an intuitive appeal to the idea of hairstyles being used to signal membership of particular social groups. The contemporary world is positively overflowing with examples of hair functioning in just such an emblematic way: consider the mohawk, the shaven head, or the afro, for instance (fig. 8). Moreover, recent work on Asian cultures has broadly supported this model.[14] However, does this necessarily mean that there is a conscious relationship between short hair and social inclusion? More nuanced studies have shown that while hair seems to be important in many diverse societies, it is not consistently or predictably manipulated with reference to a given meaning. Thus, it is perhaps more likely that hair simply represents a visible, accessible and easily manipulated medium for the display of identity, something which may include aspects of rebellion or conservatism. In this sense, it is arguably no different to any article of clothing or personal accessory.

However, this is not quite right. It does seem that hair is *particularly* closely bound up with personal identity. Anthropological support for this notion comes from the frequent use of head hair in magical rituals, wherein it comes to represent the person from which it was taken. The reasons for this may be that hair represents a particular vitality, given its relative abundance and rapid growth, and that it is seen as an extension of the person.[15] Such person–hair associations are well evidenced both in prehistory and in contemporary non-western society.[16]

The ideas discussed above constitute just a few of the ways in which scholars have attempted to interpret the diverse 'hair behaviour' that we see across time and space, throughout the human experience. Indeed, the more societies we look at, the more particularities of practice we observe, and the more difficult it becomes to pin down a single, monolithic meaning for hair. Perhaps the most important point is that hair is a far more complex medium than many would readily acknowledge. Hair itself, as well as choices about how to treat, dress or wear it are clearly laden with meaning, but that meaning is highly mutable, and depends upon social context. Analogy then takes us so far; we can propose that hair probably did have a particular significance in the Viking Age, but we are arguably no closer to identifying what that meaning was, or from where it stemmed.

8. Contemporary hairstyling: what associations do these different styles have for you? (Drawing by Steve Ashby)

Hair and Archaeology

Relative to its popularity as the subject of anthropological discussion, archaeological engagement with the topic of hair has been sparse. I don't think it is possible to entirely explain this away in terms of material preservation, though this is clearly a contributing factor.[17] However, recent years have seen signs of a movement towards engaging with this important topic, particularly in the ideas bound up with 'archaeologies of the body'.[18] Nonetheless, in the last decade or so, only one high-profile article on the archaeology of hair has been published in English: Miranda Aldhouse Green's 'Crowning Glories'.[19]

In this important article, Aldhouse-Green draws upon ethnographic, documentary and iconographic sources, as well as preserved hair remains, bog bodies and toilet instruments, in order to access the significance of hair in later prehistoric Europe. She argues that hair may have played an important role in ritual, and in the marking of boundaries between social groups and stages of life. At root, she sees hair as symbolic, something of a language; this is an interesting approach, but not the one adopted herein. I worry that if we see hair only in terms of signs and symbols, then we may become drawn to focusing too much on the more visible, more spectacular of 'hair displays': the ornate coiffures that adorn women in Roman art,[20] or the mysterious hair treatments associated with ritual sacrifice.[21] Most of the things we do with our hair are, of course, much more mundane. But that is not to say that they are not meaningful; as we have seen, many of our everyday routines are socially complex, rituals in their own right. It is simply to say that we need to find a more subtle way of explaining hair behaviour, one that accounts not just for the loud, public performances of identity recorded in art and literature, but also for the more understated activities that tend to take place in private and are rarely reflected upon, even by their practitioners.

One way of accessing such subtlety is through viewing hair behaviour as a *technology*. Following anthropologists such as Tim Ingold, many features of everyday life – walking, talking, or, in our case, personal grooming – can be seen as technologies. That is to say that they consist of skilled practice; they are techniques that are learned, and they are learned within a particular social context and environment. Thus, the way in which we walk, talk, dress and behave develop out of the experience of doing these very things within our own social world, we see how people around us behave, and we (consciously or unconsciously) mimic them.[22] This is why children develop accents, and why different fashions take hold in different places, and it goes some way to explaining why different societies have different attitudes towards work, sport, gender roles and politics. So, just as social context

9. The toolkit of contemporary haircare ritual. (Image by Alison Leonard)

influences the ways in which a craftsman goes about making a comb, on another level, context gives rise to different attitudes to grooming and personal appearance, and is thus responsible for the innovation that led to the production of composite combs in the first place, to the different roles they may have played in the British Isles, Scandinavia and further afield, and how these may have changed over time. We can learn much about this from studies of hair behaviour today, and important recent sociological studies have shown how hair behaviour can be seen as a sort of social *practice* (see fig. 9). That is to say that in the modern world, the process of 'doing your hair' can be as important as its ultimate appearance.[23] We need to take these insights on board if we are to really understand Viking-Age combs. To get at why they were important, we need to think not just about the objects in themselves, but about hair, about its role in social display, and about the practice of grooming in itself.

   To summarise then, there are many models for the understanding of hair behaviour, and many diverse associated significances; though hair seems to have held almost ubiquitous social importance, its meaning is not fixed but flexible: mutable and multifaceted.[24] It has meaning in terms of power, identity, gender, sexuality, and social inclusion or resistance.[25] One could list any number of historical contexts in which hair seems to have attained symbolic meaning. As we have seen, several mid-twentieth-century historians, anthropologists and sociologists did just that.[26] For instance, we have discussed how Leach stressed the role of hair in representing magical power, royalty, divinity and fertility, and while other ethnographers have published alternative views, they nonetheless tend to see hair as important and meaningful.[27] For example, some have seen haircutting as ritual sacrifice, while others have viewed it merely as a particularly useful field for the display of social position and inclusion.[28] While mid-twentieth-century anthropologists argued that these widespread, but broadly similar, examples suggested that hair had genuine inherent meaning, today many would suggest that the generalising covering laws necessary to support such a statement are untenable. Moreover, static, semiotic interpretations have little explanatory power. We need to appreciate that head hair represents one of the body's most easily accessible and adaptable media for expression, that it has an agency of its own and that engagement with it involves a complex canon of cultural knowledge, experience, skills, experiences and emotions. As such, its maintenance and wearing is best seen as a technology or form of practice.

It remains, then, to envisage in a little more detail how this medium was exploited in the context of Viking-Age Europe, before we move on to consider the role played by the comb in this scenario. In order to discern if our practice and technology models might be easily applied or adapted to the situation in Viking-Age Europe, we now need to focus in detail on the material, iconographic and documentary evidence from the period.

Early Medieval Hair
Before we embark upon our tour of Viking haircare in earnest, we need to consider its genesis. The production of elaborate composite combs did not spring up, unannounced, in the ninth century, and neither did the concern with presentation of hair that was their corollary. Rather, as we will see, the appearance of combs in the late third and fourth centuries was very much embedded in ideas about the articulation of hair and personal and group identity. Over the succeeding centuries, these relationships were subject to multiple transformations, and often swiftly so. Moreover, these shifts took place in accordance with more than simple fashion, but were implicated in changing ideas about status and allegiance, ethnicity and belonging, religion and political emulation. As a result, there is no simple way to consider what combs and hair 'meant', but rather we need to appreciate the innumerable shifts in association, scale and perspective that took place through the early medieval period. In what follows, in an attempt to access some of these dynamics, we will focus upon a few of the more tangible expressions of the articulation between hair and social structure, with a view to the means by which such situations could mutate into new readings of this relationship. Evidence comes from documentary, literary, iconographic, and archaeological sources.

There is no space in a book of this size to recount the history of human attitudes to hair, grooming and personal appearance. Nonetheless, it may prove instructive to briefly take a visit to early prehistory, to see if we can trace the origins and development of these ideas. As far back as the Palaeolithic, where evidence of humans, and human-like primates, is scarce, we nonetheless have tantalising glimpses of the beginnings of a concern with appearance. In the nineteenth century, cave explorers in south-west France came upon a beautifully worked ivory sculpture, showing a human head in wonderfully naturalistic detail (fig. 10). This bust, now often referred to as the 'Venus of Brassempouy', dates to the Upper Palaeolithic period (approximately 25,000 years ago), and exhibits careful attention to detail in decorative carving on the figure's crown, and around its hairline.[29] This may represent some form of hood or headdress, or, perhaps, a carefully prepared hairstyle. Either way, it shows a considerable concern with personal appearance and its representation in art, at an early stage in human social development.

It has even been argued that grooming itself played a fundamental role in early human evolution, and in the development of language in particular. Robin Dunbar showed that most of our communication is not about the delivery of important information (about food, breeding or danger, for instance), but is rather mundane, and is chiefly concerned with

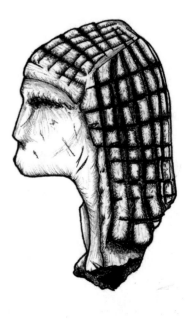

10. The 'Venus of Brassempouy'. (Drawing by Hayley Saul)

maintaining connections between people.[30] He suggested that it fulfils a similar purpose to that played by grooming behaviour in ape communities, and that speech may even have developed as a means of maintaining social contact in new environments and communities that made constant physical engagement difficult. If this is true – and I believe it's a compelling case – then humans have a very deep-seated concern with grooming. The process is important in itself as a way of maintaining intimacy, of regulating individual behaviour and group dynamics, and of creating relationships between people. Perhaps it should be no surprise that thousands of years later, people were investing so much time in the production, trade and maintenance of hair combs, no matter how mundane they may seem to us today.

But there may be more to it than that. I suspect that, as well as having its roots in the structuring of social relationships through intimate physical contact, grooming betrays a basic human concern with physical appearance, and the way in which the self is displayed to others. This is clearly manifested in the Venus of Brassempouy, while later in the Stone Age, the frequent association of flint blades with burials might suggest that they were valued as razors, and it has even been suggested that Neolithic 'thumbnail scrapers' may have been carried as a functional tool intended for use on the body.[31] By the Bronze Age, tweezers and razors were important parts of the personal toolkit, and many of them were highly decorated, suggesting that they were highly prized items. This concern with the body is even clearer in other parts of the globe; by the Bronze Age, the world was starting to see the development of complex civilisation in the Near East and Mediterranean, and the considerable material records of Ancient Egypt and Greece provide key documents for our understanding of past attitudes to personal appearance.

In Egypt, for example, where clothing (for many) was relatively simple, hair was a particularly important social indicator.[32] Irrespective of social standing, hair was an important field for social display, to the extent that we see both men and women wearing hair extensions and wigs,[33] and that there were royal wigmakers and hairdressers. Priests removed all of their body hair ahead of important rituals, and thus wore wigs at other times, while in the secular world wigs even seem to have picked up an erotic significance, as there are several references to people putting their wigs *on* before sex. These ideas might seem a little alien in their detail, but they evidence a common concern with personal display, and provide yet more examples of the ways in which hair may act as an active player in the construction of identities. Indeed, Robins[34] has argued that the relationships between hairstyle, status, gender and life stage were strictly proscribed, and even if these associations are not at first clear to us, they would have been well understood within their own particular context. Hair had been appropriated as a medium of power.

Back in western Europe, in the Iron Age we see evidence of a continuing concern with the ritual of grooming. Mirrors (fig. 11) from this period constitute beautiful works of art, although these might be interpreted in magical, cosmological or eschatological terms; they may have played a role in divination.[35] It is more difficult to see such a role for combs and shears (fig. 12). In Britain, the later Iron Age and Roman periods see a growth in the corpus of material culture associated with personal appearance, including mortars and pestles for the preparation of cosmetics, toilet sets including ear scoops and nail cleaners, pins for the dressing of hair and (perhaps) ocular application of kohl, and ultimately the composite hair combs. It is noteworthy that these are frequently well-made, even decorative objects, often used as elements of dress in themselves; in Roman Britain in particular, a concern with personal appearance was something to be proud of, and its material culture constituted an important component of civilised Roman identity.

Indeed, Roman commentators seem to have been more than a little preoccupied with appearance, and their descriptions of the 'barbarians' against which they judged themselves are frequently pitched in terms of personal appearance, often making reference to the hairstyles and bodypainting or tattooing of Germanic, Celtic and other European peoples.[36] Thus, while bathing and toilet ritual was fundamental to the practice of 'being Roman', the satirical poet Juvenal refers to barbarians as being 'untouched by the comb'. This, while supporting the contention that grooming and appearance were central to the idea of *Romanitas*, to 'civilised' Roman society, does not mean that hair was insignificant to the 'barbarians', only that it was employed in different ways. Indeed, while Roman appearance and grooming behaviours were strictly controlled (in the army, in particular, a uniform appearance helped to construct a sense of collective identity[37]), the 'barbarians' of northern Europe were not quite as wild and unkempt as Roman commentators would have us believe, and hair and appearance were actually important parts of the identity of many of the tribes that lay beyond Caesar's reach.[38] For example, images of Theoderic, even if otherwise dressing him in the regalia of a Roman ruler, proudly display his long, curly hair as an important signifier of his non-Roman roots.[39]

Tacitus reports that in certain Germanic tribes, adolescent males were not permitted to trim their head or facial hair until they had successfully made a human kill;[40] this is a clear indicator that hair was being used to establish social standing and life stage, and that it was bound up within

11. An Iron-Age mirror from Desborough, Northamptonshire. (Drawing by Nick Griffiths)

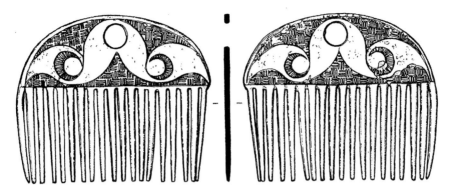

12. An Iron-Age comb from Tanworth-in-Arden, Warks. (Drawing by Candy Stevens)

a broader social and moral code. Indeed, much as Roman commentators are wont to speak of the wild appearance of barbarian tribes, we should realise that any such hirsuteness represented a conscious decision, rather than a lack of concern with personal display. Moreover, long hair does not mean *unstyled* hair, and there are indications that the various Germanic tribes curated discrete ways of dressing their hair, in order to differentiate themselves from each other and to distinguish male from female, freeman from slave. They also seem to have treated their hair with a range of natural products and dyes,[41] and it is very clear that the idea of 'barbarian haircare' is far from the oxymoron it may superficially appear to be.[42]

As the historian Paul Dutton has written, the situation can be explained as follows. For the Germanic peoples, the length, style and appearance of hair were key to social communication and the maintenance of hierarchy and gender relations. To the Roman commentator, it was easy and convenient to explain away this dependence on a complex array of hair-borne social markers as the trappings of a dirty, unkempt, uncivilised, inferior – but nonetheless dangerous – Other. This can clearly be seen in the fact that Germanic submission to Roman dominance frequently took the form of shaving and head shearing.[43] Hair then, because of the different ways in which it was conceived of and manipulated in these disparate cultures, became a key marker of social distinction: on one level, hairstyle could be used to mark out man from woman, old from young, free from unfree and tribe from tribe, but on a much cruder level all this diversity could be packaged up as the 'hairiness' of the barbarian, distinct from the 'civilised', closely shorn head of the Roman citizen.

Against the backdrop of imperial Rome, the Germanic preference for long hair left a significant legacy. Indeed, it is probably in early medieval continental Europe that we see the most striking evidence for a social and political concern with personal appearance, and with head and facial hair in particular. Neither is this association restricted to Germanic groups, as iconographic evidence on the early medieval symbol stones of Scotland suggests that combs held a particular symbolic significance in Pictish art and society. Moreover, these same forms of sculpture suggest that hairstyle itself was used to mark out status, and it is notable that the famous stone from the Brough of Birsay in Orkney depicts a group of warriors whose leader is differentiated most clearly through difference of hairstyle.

These 'Celtic' examples notwithstanding, the significance of grooming is most clearly discernible in the societies that developed out of the old 'Barbarian cultures'. We can see this in the Anglo-Saxon attachment to the comb; for a group popularly conceived of as wild and unkempt, they do seem to have invested this piece of grooming equipment with a particular significance. Not only did the Germanic peoples of late and post-Roman Europe develop their own forms of comb (they were probably actually responsible for the innovation of the composite comb that was taken up in Roman Britain), but these objects clearly held ritual or magical power, given their privileged place in burial practice. Indeed, Anglo-Saxon funerary practice suggests a special functional and symbolic role for hair combs in the transformation of the body,[44] while the famous tombstone from Niederdollendorf (fig. 13) depicts a warrior in the very act of combing his hair; in this piece of iconography, it is difficult to argue against the comb representing as significant a component of the image as the more traditional foci of academic study, such as his sword.[45]

Moreover, in Merovingian (mid-fifth- to mid-eighth-century) Frankia, hair seems to have taken on a heightened significance in the marking of social status and negotiation of hierarchy.[46] Long hair, in particular, was important on a number of levels: it stood for elite status, for freedom, for ethnicity (and what we might term *Germanitas*). It was illegal for a slave to wear a wig, and illegal to cut off the hair of a freeborn child without their guardians' say-so, such was the strength of the connection between hair and social standing.[47] To care for one's hair was in itself an indicator of status; to do so was a luxury restricted to certain levels of society. Moreover, while the free differentiated themselves from the unfree by means of their unshorn hair, truly *long* hair was a closely guarded marker of royalty, and may have been deemed somehow imbued with magical power, itself the root of royal status.[48] Members of the Merovingian dynasty reputedly grew their hair long from childhood, combing and otherwise carefully managing it as a symbol of their status. It is thus notable that the artistic treatment of hair is one of the most remarkable features of Merovingian coins;[49] it was important that this image was widely disseminated among the subjects of the realm, and beyond. The significance of 'elite hair' is

13. The Niederdollendorf Stone, Germany. Note sword (passive) and comb (active). (Drawing by Hayley Saul)

pressed into even starker relief in accounts of the shearing of royal captives, and the tonsuring of freemen in order to relieve them of their property.[50] Such 'hair abuse' constituted a form of torture with important symbolic content; it humiliated the subject, marking them out as socially and politically impotent. No doubt this understanding lies at the root of religious tonsuring; upon entering the church, the removal of hair symbolises the renunciation not just of material wealth, but also of political status. Or at least this was the theory. Whether hair's central role in the maintenance of social hierarchy stems from 'pagan' ideas, or whether it is more bound up with early Christian tradition (such as the story of Samson) is subject to some debate,[51] but for us, the symbolic justification is in some ways unimportant; the key idea is that it *was* socially and politically significant.

In the succeeding era of Carolingian dominance, hair was given up to one's superiors as a sign of submission borne of Roman ideals, and short hair ultimately came to replace flowing locks as the desirable style, drawing new (or at least different) connections with Christianity and ideas of Romanitas. Facial hair also became important, as Charlemagne's own moustache was used as a visual cue to draw associations with Theoderic, the great Ostrogothic hero of the 'barbarians'. However, it has to be pointed out that just because the Carolingian kings had rejected the Merovingian belief in 'hair magic', it does not follow that hair was unimportant to them; rather, their active choice in this matter signifies quite the opposite.[52] In addition, in adjacent areas of northern Europe, long hair may still have been prized.[53] Faced with the long hair of Scandinavians, for instance, perhaps the shorn heads of the Carolingian kings allowed them to feel distinctive and superior, not least because it harked back to that old Roman–barbarian dichotomy.

Thus, in pagan Scandinavia, and more particularly in the complex melting pot that was late ninth- and tenth-century Britain, there was immense potential for arguments concerning social status, ethnicity, gender and life stage to be played out through the medium of hair. Particular evidence for the meaningful employment of hair in Viking-Age northern Europe comes from archaeological, written (literary and historical) and iconographic sources. These will be considered in turn below.

Viking Hair: Archaeological Evidence

Though the archaeological record from ninth to eleventh-century northern Europe is rather patchy, and is not generally informative with regard to hair behaviour, there are a few exceptions. We have a range of sources to consider, from the combs themselves, to preserved remains of hair, to artistic representations that feature hair and grooming. Direct archaeological evidence of the significance of hair comes from locks placed in a Viking-Age grave at Skoppinstull, Hovgården, in Adelsö parish in Uppland, Sweden.[54] This find is echoed by a number of occurrences of locks of hair among grave goods; see, for example, the braids from a burial mound in Efaefsk, Russia.[55] In the context of its use in magic and shamanism, hair may be seen as an extension of the person (see below), and it may not be unreasonable to view such depositions in this way. However, given the degradable nature of hair, such instances are rare. More common is the interment of combs, and the analysis of such contexts may be a more fruitful avenue into comprehending any magical or cosmological significances associated with hair. This will be discussed more fully in Chapter 5, but now we'll turn to documentary, literary and art historical sources.

Viking Hair: The Written Evidence

Given the dearth of written sources for this period, it is not feasible to completely bypass non-contemporary or geographically displaced evidence. For example, while the Icelandic sagas (from which much of the historian's knowledge of Viking-Age Scotland has been drawn) are not contemporary for the earliest periods of Scandinavian settlement in Britain, they remain useful sources when studied critically.[56]

Recent work on medieval European documentary sources makes a number of important connections clear: between hair and status, ethnicity, age, sex (being particularly important in complex definitions of gender) and morality.[57] It is also interesting to note that hair may be manipulated in order to negotiate and move between different proscribed categories (a form of 'disguise'). Unfortunately, Viking-Age references to hair are conspicuously absent from such discussions. This reflects the paucity of surviving written sources for the period (a particular problem in the north). Nonetheless, we do have a number of contemporary references to go on. These tend to come from the point of view of 'outsiders' to the Scandinavian world; Anglo-Saxon clerics, or travellers from the east in particular.

An Eastern Perspective

We opened this chapter with an extract from Ibn Fadlan's famous account of the rites and traditions of the Rus. This perhaps requires a little context. On a visit to the Volga area, Ibn Fadlan, ambassadorial secretary to the Abbasid caliphate, came into contact with this ethnically complex group (but which indubitably incorporated a strong Scandinavian component). In his account, he describes – with some distaste – the Rus' daily, communal habit of washing and combing their hair.

On first reading, the account flies in the face of any attempt to argue that Viking-Age Scandinavians took their hair seriously. However, it is important to see the quote within its context; Ibn Fadlan, as an aristocratic Muslim studying an alien people, was not without agenda, and may well have intended to emphasise the uncleanliness of the alien peoples with whom he made contact. However, even if the passage exaggerates the communality of this daily ritual, it does undermine any idea of hair maintenance as part of a private toilet. At least in this context, we may rather see it as a ritual intended to reinforce family and peer group ties.

European Perspectives

On another level, Ibn Fadlan's reaction reminds us of the possibility that hair behaviour may be an important field for the expression of identity. Further examples are provided by repeated references in saga to the strangeness of the hairstyles of priests encountered in the British Isles,[58] and in other early medieval sources such as Adam of Bremen's *History of the Archbishops of Hamburg-Bremen*.[59] In these documents, explicit connections are made between group identity and hair colour, style, headwear and clothing. Indeed, 'hairstyles and body signs' are one of four areas (along with language, weaponry and military tactics, and costume) that the historian Walter Pohl famously singled out as important in strategies used in the expression of ethnicity.[60]

These examples notwithstanding, it is clear that strictly contemporary sources are sparse, and it seems germane to examine the Icelandic sagas. If we assume for the moment that these sources have some broad relevance for the Viking Age (in that they probably share certain literary and story-telling traditions, and a common mythology, if not in terms of being an accurate record of historical events), then it is notable that they contain a number of references to hair. Indeed, it is one of the primary characteristics used in the somewhat formulaic manner in which key figures are described in the texts, while qualities of the hair are often incorporated into characters' nicknames.[61] The most famous example of this application is the case of King Harald Harfager (translation: Finehair/ Fairhear) of Norway, whom we have already discussed in brief. When he finally becomes ruler of Norway, Harald turns his attention to his hair, and in the most evocative manner:

Now King Harald was a-feasting in Mere at Earl Rognvald's, and had now gotten to him all the land. So King Harald took a bath, and then he let his hair be combed, and then Earl Rognvald sheared it. And heretofore it had been unshorn and uncombed for ten winters. Aforetime he had been called Shock-head, but now Earl Rognvald gave him a by-name

and called him Harald Hairfair, and all said who saw him that that was
smoothly named, for he had both plenteous hair and goodly.

Heimskringla: Harald Harfager's Saga, Chapter 23[62]

This idea echoes the oath of Julius Civilis (the leader of the Batavian
revolt against Rome in AD 69) to grow his hair until he had defeated the
legions.[63] Though there is certainly an element of trope in both examples,
this does little to diminish the power of the image; it must have been a
relationship that was understood, at least in aristocratic circles, in both of
these contexts, separated though they were by a millennium.

As a literary device, long, luxuriant hair is frequently proposed as an
attribute of beauty – and, arguably, is an indirect indicator of virtue – in
both men and women.[64] Of all the examples of this device, the references
from the *Edda* are particularly noteworthy.[65] The Aesir, the mythical
(ostensibly Trojan) god-ancestors of the peoples of medieval Scandinavia,
are each described, frequently with reference to the beauty of their hair.
Such tropes obviously have an origin in everyday attitudes to beauty and
personal appearance, and there is some evidence to suggest that hair was
seen as an important secondary sexual feature in the Viking Age and/or
medieval period; in one passage from a saga, this seems to be a factor in
the acquisiton of female slaves:

> The only captives from the fray
> Were lovely maidens led away.
> And in wild terror to the strand,
> Down to the ships, the linked band
> Of fair-haired girls is roughly driven
> Their soft skins by the irons riven.

Heimskringla, the Saga of
Harald Hardrada, Chapter 19[66]

This idea of hair as a signifier of beauty is mirrored in Bede's famous
account of the charm of Anglian slaves,[67] while in court circles, the
importance of hair in attraction also seems to have been marked; King
Magnus Barefoot referred in verse to his wife-to-be as 'the lovely one with
light-brown hair'.[68] Again, these are clearly tropes, but that is not to say
that they fail to reflect more widely understood hair-related associations.

Moreover, the different qualities of hair seem to have particular
significances. Thus, grey or white hair is often used to symbolise great age,
frailness or wisdom. Indeed, this rather intuitive literary device can be traced
back to at least the sixth century (see *The Gododdin*, and texts by Taliesin),
although there is, of course, no need to posit a common tradition.

If greying, or balding hair can be seen to represent the old and weak, or the wise, what does a full head of hair mean? The repeated use of insults such as 'no beard' and 'dungbeard' in *Njal's Saga* certainly suggest that male facial hair had some role as an indicator of maturity or masculinity.[69] Could head hair perhaps make particular reference to life and vitality, and might it have magical properties? A few passages from sagas do support such a supposition. Also in *Njal's Saga*,[70] Gunnar asks his wife Hallgerda to twist locks of her hair together to form a bowstring that will protect him in battle, while in *The Tale of Audun from the West Fjords*,[71] when Audun loses his health and good fortune while returning from pilgrimage, he also loses his hair and becomes miserable. In Saxo Grammaticus's *Gesta Danorum*, the hair of giants is singled out for attention, and its plucking seems to hold particular symbolic significance.[72]

There are also numerous references to hair within the context of warfare – arguably supporting the idea that it was seen as the seat of life and vitality. Sagas refer to 'cleaving hair, together with head and helmet', in *Heimskringla*,[73] the bloodying of hair in battle,[74] the (probably related) hiding of hair under helmets,[75] and the request of Sigurd, Boe's son, not to get his hair bloody upon his decapitation.[76] All this might suggest some idea of power or life being bound up in the hair, and perhaps that its bloodying or cutting would be seen as detrimental or disgraceful. Such an idea of hair as a symbol of life and vitality is supported by the story of the incorruption of St Olaf's body after death, a subject that receives extensive treatment in *Heimskringla*. We are told that on opening his casket, Bishop Grimkel and other observers were faced not just by a 'glorious fragrance', but also by the sight of St Olaf's face, unchanged since death, and of his hair and nails having grown. The bishop then sheared Olaf's hair and trimmed his beard, and that which was removed was pronounced a holy relic. They then proceeded to test the power of this relic; the story continues:

> Then the bishop let take fire in a censer, and blessed it and laid incense thereon, and sithence laid on the fire the hair of King Olaf; and when all the incense was burnt out, the bishop took the hair out of the fire, and then was the hair unburnt ... And so the bishop declared, and the king assented thereto, and all the folk judged, that King Olaf was verily a holy man.
>
> *Heimskringla, The Story of Olaf the Holy,*
> *the Son of Harald*, Chapter 258[77]

It is interesting that the qualities of St Olaf's hair were seen as so central to his holiness. Moreover, the sagas go on to say that the growth of his hair and nails continued for some time afterwards, and that an effort was made to trim them periodically. One might draw parallels with the pagan Scandinavian tradition – according to the *Edda* – in which it was important not to die with uncut fingernails, as they would play a pivotal role in Ragnarök.[78] The perceived seriousness of dirtying and maltreatment of hair might equally relate to a perceived injury of honour, perhaps echoing ideas from Merovingian Frankia. Stories of 'hair abuse' may support this; one is drawn, for instance, to the events recorded by Saxo Grammaticus, when a giant causes the hair of his captive, Siritha, to become knotted and horny. This is seen as a particularly shameful act of neglect and cruelty. Interestingly, the same text contains references to the pulling and burning of hair as acts of torture, and given the prevalence of the theme, it is difficult not to read a symbolic dimension into the recounting of such instances of 'hair abuse'.[79]

So, in the formulaic world of medieval Norse history, saga and poetry, hair may be employed to signify power, vitality, age, youth, strength, wisdom or beauty. If the literature can be taken as a reflection of more widely held beliefs and attitudes (which, admittedly, given the timelapse in their transcription, is far from assured), then we may suggest that a number of Viking-Age character stereotypes incorporated particular hair attributes. These related not just to *quality* of hair, however, but also to particular *ways of wearing* that were appropriate to certain demographic groups, or certain occasions. Thus, Saxo Grammaticus repeatedly lends his opinion on the appropriateness of styles of hairdressing for battle. More generally, loose hair is often taken as a sign of youthful abandon (see above). This connection is paralleled in the symbolic treatment of facial hair; beards receive significant attention in early medieval literature,[80] and it is tempting to view such allusions as manifestations of a symbolic link between beard growth and maturity, experience and wisdom. However, whether such literary devices betray any more widespread mental connections is difficult to ascertain, and it would be dangerous to uncritically extrapolate saga references back into the ninth and tenth centuries.

It may be that it was seen as respectable for married women to tie up or dress their hair; there are repeated references to such behaviour, as well as transgressions from the norm, in both Saxon and Norse literature.[81] Headdresses, hoods, veils and hats are occasionally alluded to, the former frequently as items of status, and it may be of note that one particularly ostentatious headdress – with its connections to family and loyalty – brings about the dispute that is core to the narrative of *The Saga of the People of Laxardal*.[82] It is tempting to read this as evidence of the centrality of hair behaviour to the construction of identity, and of the ways in which the material culture caught up in such behaviour could be invested with qualities of kinship, loyalty and trust. Indeed, archaeologists have recently suggested that bonds of kinship (secured through rituals of birth and death, marriage and inheritance) needed to be materialised in some way, and that portable items played a central role as gifts in this process. It has even been argued that this particular use of precious metal items lay at the heart of the whole Viking expansion; the need to secure bridewealth led to raiding overseas, while the growth of industry at market centres may also have been focused on this particular market, at least initially.[83] The sagas suggest that, just like jewellery, headdresses played a role in such tradition, so why not combs too, particularly when they were made and sold at the same places as the oval brooches, glass beads and other personal adornments that we associate with marriage gifts? Like jewellery, they are decorative objects into which much manufacturing effort is invested, and like jewellery they are frequently found in graves. Moreover, they are, as we will see, at least equally implicated in the production and maintenance of personal and social identity. Their role in styling hair, and thus in ensuring that personal appearance signified precisely what it was meant to in social terms, saw to this. We could say that combs were active players in the policing of social practice.

Hair in Anglo-Saxon and 'Celtic' Sources

Much of the evidence referred to above comes from Old Norse literature, but while we may suggest that this preserves a Viking-Age Scandinavian tradition, it is of course separated in time from the context it describes by several centuries, which might lead us to question its validity in this sense. We do have a number of contemporary documents – chronicles, hagiographies and poems set down in the Viking Age itself – but they are subject to a different bias: the world view of the clergy. Nonetheless, the thoughts and works of Anglo-Saxon and Celtic priests and monks are of some interest, and their views of the role hair played in both 'heathen' and 'Christian' societies may be enlightening.

If we accept the idea that hair was seen as in some way symbolic of a person's spirit of life and vitality, we might ask how perceptions of hair developed with the growth in popularity of Christianity. Was 'hair imagery' an important part of early Christian teaching and myth? There are some obvious examples from the writings of the Christian church in Britain. Locks ostensibly taken from the hair of saints seem to have been a popular relic. For example, Bede states that a lock of St Cuthbert's hair had healing powers.[84] A point of caution must be made, however. The importance of hair in Christian symbolism cannot have been all-pervasive in early medieval Britain, and there is a notable absence of references to hair treatment in monastic customaries (manuals for the proper observance of

St Benedict's *Rule*).[85] Hair behaviour had important symbolic associations, and was clearly a mediator in a wide range of social negotiations, but it was one of many such mechanisms.

Nonetheless, it might be significant that references to hair, its care and dressing can be found in Saxon documentary sources that we might otherwise expect to overlook such trivialities.[86] The English chronicler John of Wallingford petitions against the imitation of Scandinavian hair behaviour,[87] while, as we have seen at the top of the chapter, in his famous letter to Aethelred of Northumbria following the raid of Lindisfarne, Alcuin is equally forthright on the matter. This apparent English admiration of Scandinavian grooming is instructive in a number of ways (quite apart from the striking contrast with Ibn Fadlan's rather disparaging views of Rus hair behaviour). The Church's attempts to suppress such imitation is interesting in that it constitutes evidence that hair could be used as a field for the expression of identity. The reasons for John of Wallingford and Alcuin's protestations are complex and elusive. However, in many contexts a particular focus for religious writers seems to be a more or less explicit connection between hair grooming and piety, and one can certainly imagine ninth-century Scandinavian hairdos being characterised by the clergy as 'pagan'. Indeed, the connection between hair and religious devotion is not a fanciful one, and the issue of appropriately 'pious hair' (whether groomed, or devoutly uncared for) was far from trivial. The role of monastic tonsure, and its proper character (i.e. that of St Peter, rather than the Simoniac or Irish variants),[88] was an issue of considerable import throughout the early medieval period (fig. 14). It is a particular concern

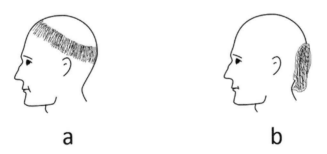

a   b

14. Haircuts of contention: the (a) Roman and (b) Celtic tonsures. (Drawing by Steve Ashby after Venclová 2002)

of Bede, and along with the accepted date for Easter, was responsible for one of the major areas of disagreements between the churches of Rome and Ireland.[89] We won't go into the detail of this here, but, if we needed any more evidence, this fact demonstrates very clearly that hair, and its treatment, were certainly not seen as trivial concerns in early medieval society.

Technology and Practice

Our survey of the anthropology and sociology of 'hair behaviours' has made one thing abundantly clear: there is no one social meaning for hair, no single rationale for the resources and effort invested in its manipulation. Rather, meaning emerges from context. Given the fragmentary nature of the archaeological evidence for hair and its treatment in the Viking Age, it is difficult to identify its particular significance in this context. However, what we *can* do is consider the framework within which hair behaviour develops. We don't need to know its precise 'meaning' (if any such thing exists) to be able to understand a little about the role it plays in the structuring of relations, and what its social power is. Thus, we might never be able to say what a ninth-century king thought that his hair stood for or 'meant', but we can say that a concern with hair and its treatment was central to the negotiation of social boundaries; the lines that defined demographic groups – ethnicity, gender, kinship, status – were drawn in hair. Moreover, its manipulation played an important part in crossing these lines, hence the careful policing of hairstyles in Merovingian Frankia, and the concern of Christian commentators in early Viking-Age England.

Thus, it is important to think about hair as a practice, even a process, rather than simply as a medium, a sort of bodily object. If we focus on the dressing and wearing of hair as a practice, one begun in private, and then performed in public, it will allow us to avoid seeing hair only in turns of the *semiotics* or symbolic meaning of hair, and to avoid paying too much attention to the (relatively rare) spectacular hair-based expressions of identity. Instead, it finds meaning in the everyday, mundane aspects of hair 'ritual'. Hairdressing is thus not simply about fashion, about very overt, deliberate expressions of identity, but rather about maintenance and awareness of the self. We find meaning in the ways that people go about looking after and seeing to their hair, whether or not they actively *believe* that what they are doing is significant.[90]

So how can we do this? Recent studies of hair behaviour in the modern world can give us a good start.[91] The first thing to do is to think about the particularities of hair; what makes hair different from dress, for example?

How can we define *hair behaviour*? There are a number of key points to consider.

First, hair is a living structure, rather than an inert object. Its role in display is thus very different, and very much more complex than that of an artefact such as a brooch, a hat, a sword. Our relationship with hair is complex; it is alive when in the head, and dead when out of it. It is very clearly a part of us in the former case, and separate from us in the latter (though, some element of our 'essence' is apparently retained even in shed hair, hence its utility in magic and witchcraft). More simply, the fact that hair is alive means that it doesn't always behave as it should.[92] This superficially rather obvious point is one easily overlooked by archaeologists, anthropologists, and sociologists alike. We talk of how hair is used to communicate, to deliver messages, to display affiliation or indicate life stage. But if it refuses to be manipulated in the manner its wearer intends, but rather proves resistant (as practical experience tells us it frequently does) what then? The fact that hair *cannot* be perfectly sculpted actually lends it its complexity and power. It is the act of preparation, rather than its final appearance that is key; the social significance of hair lies in *performance*, rather than in appearance.

Nonetheless, such performance would be futile if there were not some means of at least approximating a particular 'look'. Managing this negotiation between an individual's vision of a particular hairstyle and the real-world restrictions of hair type, condition and climate is dependent on the particular skill set of the stylist. Indeed, a range of skills, competences and emotions are involved. It is also tied up with other practices, such as dressing or bathing, and particular people, relationships, times and social contexts. Thus, specific occasions, audiences and places may become particularly significant in the performance of dressing and wearing hair; the process is not divorced from the world in which it takes place. In the modern world, it has been shown that haircare is primarily about appearance, and about tactile sensation. It might, therefore, be distinguished from bathing, which is justified in terms of cleanliness, smell and the refreshing of the body.[93] How much cleaning of the body is necessary, and how much time we spend on the styling of hair, is not 'natural', but is socially proscribed. Today, we shower more than we used to (for many years wetting the hair was seen as unhealthy, and to be avoided), and while we consider the natural greasiness of unwashed hair undesirable, we replace it with artificial grease in the form of waxes, gels and creams. It might thus be suggested that we implicitly believe in 'good' and 'bad' forms of dirt.[94] In short, our relationship with our hair, and the things we think we need to do to it, are complex, and socially specific. Studies of contemporary attitudes to hair (above) are thus invaluable in getting to the bottom of the relationship between individuals and their hair in the Viking Age.

Thankfully, we also have a few material items to work with: combs. As well as a particular skill set, a range of paraphernalia is always involved in haircare. Today, we may use combs and brushes, hairdryers and tongs, gels and sprays. Options in the Viking Age may appear comparatively limited, but one may nonetheless envision the use of combs and pins, as well as 'products' such as dyes, oils and waxes. Haircare has, and has always had, a materiality. It is combs, as the more robust elements of that materiality, which allow us to study its performance in the Viking Age.

But we must not forget that it is the performance itself that is key. We may see this performance as a sort of technology, in the same way that the anthropologist Alfred Gell talked of 'technologies of enchantment'.[95] Just as the artist may produce artefacts that do more than simply showcase their craftsmanship, but rather evoke a sense of a wonder, so the same may be true, on some level, of the hairdresser. Thus, styled hair evokes what has been done to it, speaking of the skill, effort, time and paraphernalia involved in its production and maintenance. At root, the purpose of haircare is the effect its result has on others, on the hair's 'audience'. But, as we have seen, the ultimate result is not completely controllable, and though an individual may aspire to a particular look, to signal a particular affiliation, to achieve a particular reaction, in practice it is the *process* of styling the hair which becomes important in itself. The significance of hair is in the *doing*, not the *wearing*, and identity is emergent in the striving for a particular look, rather than simply in the successful communication of that look. In short, hair is not about colours and styles, but about techniques and technologies.

Thus far we have demonstrated (1) that hair and hair behaviours hold significance in diverse contexts across space and time; (2) that early medieval literature frequently uses hair as a kind of shorthand in order to describe and situate its characters; (3) that this, together with more anecdotal reference to hair behaviour in letters and chronicles, broadly suggests that there was a concern with hair and its proper treatment in elite and (probably) non-elite society; (4) that particular ways of wearing the hair would have been seen as appropriate or inappropriate in certain contexts, such that aliens and deviants would be easily identifiable. All of this goes some way to explaining the perceived need for complex, ornate, and presumably expensive hair combs in Viking-Age society. It goes some way, but not all the way. Our next job is to construct an explanatory framework that will allow us to interpret this phenomenon in detail. Exactly why did people of influence in early medieval Europe develop such a need to maintain a well-groomed head of hair, such a need that it

15. Peacock and deer. (Images by '10mpx cg', Wikimedia Commons; and Ruth Carden)

necessitated the production of objects as complex, over-engineered and frequently elaborately decorated as the composite comb?

The first question is why the need to groom, in itself, developed and, in particular, why it developed as a badge of the free individual, and of the elite. A rather surprising analogy might be made here. It comes from the world of zoology, and a concept known as 'handicap theory'.[96]

Hair and Handicap

The tailfan of the peacock, the antlers of the deer – it is a truism to state that these play a role in sexual selection (fig. 15). We instinctively know that the stag with the largest antlers, or the peacock with the most elaborate fan, will provide the most attractive mate for the hind or the peahen. But why should this be so, when tailfans and antlers confer nothing on the individual but a massive energy drain? In fact, this paradox may actually provide a clue to their significance: antlers and tailfans provide a test of the male's quality. Only the strongest, most healthy of individuals will be able to maintain inordinately overdeveloped appendages. The very fact that certain individuals have them testifies powerfully to their desirability as a mate.

But what does this digression tell us about Vikings, their hair and their combs? I don't mean to imply a direct analogy, and the sexual element, while potentially significant, is not central here. However, it is fair to say that in pre-industrial society, only members of certain levels of society will have had the free time to spend on extravagances such as personal grooming. Thus, such activities became symbols of status in themselves. It is well known that in both Roman and medieval society, particular status was conferred on those foodstuffs that provided small quantities of meat relative to the amount of effort taken in order to hunt them (Roman aristocrats, for instance, had a penchant for dormice). Thus, the provision at feasts of such inefficiently produced foods constituted a powerful statement of wealth and elite identity: 'I had the time, skill, and resources to hunt this.'[97] Perhaps a similar situation persisted in the early medieval attitude to personal grooming; to groom was to make a statement about the pressures on your time, about what was important to you, about your free or elite status. If this seems a little far-fetched, then just note that such associations were so important to the social structure of Merovingian Frankia that they became legally codified. We may propose that similar connections were popularly understood in Viking-Age Britain and Scandinavia, even if differently expressed.

Class and Cleanliness
That is well and good, and goes some way to explaining why fundamentally optional, or even frivolous, activities became meaningfully loaded. However, it does not tell us why personal grooming in particular became socially elevated. There is any number of pastimes that only the elite may have been able to regularly practise; one might think of swordplay, reading and writing, hunting for sport, or even boardgames, perhaps. Why personal grooming?

As we have seen, hair is the most visible and easily manipulable indicator of personal identity. However, it is also a powerful and readily perceptible display of personal *cleanliness*. This seems like a fairly bland, neutral statement, until we realise that 'being clean' is not natural, objective or easily measured. Rather, *dirt* is a social construct used to separate social classes.[98] Just as Roman commentators were disparaging about their hairy, barbarian neighbours, so for centuries have members of the elite looked down upon their social subordinates as dirty, unkempt and uncivilised. Personal appearance has always been used as a means of social distinction, and while brooches and expensive dress accessories speak volumes about relative wealth, indicators of personal hygiene say something much more profound; they may be read in terms of different moral codes, different attitudes, different priorities. They are thus fundamental to the separation of *them* and *us*.

With this in mind, particularly powerful statements of identity could be made using media that allowed communication of both ethnicity/group membership and social status. Hair allowed all of this and more. It was close to eye level, and thus one of the first aspects of personal appearance that an observer would notice. Through washing, combing, cutting, colouring, greasing, styling and accessorising, it was easy to manipulate in myriad ways. Within the particular cultural parameters of a given society, it would thus be very easy to determine an individual's social standing, and outsiders (whether foreigners or other 'marginal' characters, such as criminals, slaves or the insane) would be even more easily recognised. Hair does not simply make statements about how someone looks, but also about *what has been done to the hair*. It speaks volumes about the social practices in which its wearer engages, which tell us about *who they are*. Thus, it is natural that hair became an important field for social display, and, as we will see in Chapter 5, that the tools involved in such practice themselves received an elevated social significance. In short, personal grooming was taken up as an activity that allowed the easy distinction of members of the elite, their followers and their slaves. Moreover, it allowed these distinctions to be maintained and reproduced. Haircare is not the benign, somewhat esoteric concern it may at first seem. Rather, it is politically loaded, and in the Viking Age was an important medium in the structuring of society, a key ideological tool with which the elite maintained their dominance over their subordinates. Hair was nothing less than a battleground on which to play out social dispute and power – a technology of social and economic oppression.

5

Combs and Communities

I rejoice greatly in your prosperity, and I have taken great pleasure in your loving present, giving thanks in proportion to the number of teeth I have counted in your gift. A wonderful animal with two heads and sixty teeth – not as large as an elephant, but made of beautiful ivory. I was not terrified by this beast, but was delighted by its appearance, and had no fear that it might bite me with its gnashing teeth, but I was amused by the charming servility with which it smoothed down the hair on my head. I didn't consider the ferocity of the teeth, but rather cherished the affection of the sender, which I have always found utterly reliable.

Letter from Alcuin of York to Archbishop Riculf of Mainz, *c.* 794[1]

Having considered hair behaviour in time and space, and speculated about how it may have worked in the Viking Age, in the last chapter we came to the realisation that attitudes to hair are generated out of *practice*, out of a sort of social technology. It remains, then, to consider the roles played by the tools in this technology: the combs themselves. We have attempted to explain the 'world of hair' in which composite combs operated, our next job is to consider exactly how they operated – how were they used, where, when and by whom? And just as importantly, what power did combs have to 'act back' upon the user, to communicate with other audiences, or to structure relations? We have seen that hair (as a manipulable element of the human body) had such power; what then of combs (as inanimate, ostensibly inert, but highly engineered and valued objects)? This is what theoretical archaeologists would refer to as the *materiality* of hair care. In order to address this question, we will need to consider anthropological and ethnographic work on the use of combs, before we return to the archaeological evidence itself.

Combs have been and remain objects of meaning in many cultural contexts. For example, together with the hair (*kes*; see above), the *kangha*, or comb is one of the 'Five Ks' of Sikhism,[2] while the hair comb was an important status symbol among many Polynesian peoples in the historical period.[3] With these resonances in diverse social contexts in mind, can we assume such importance in Viking-Age Britain? Given their widespread distribution, there seems little doubt that combs were important in early medieval Europe. It remains to demonstrate, however, whether their importance was primarily one of a practical, hygienic, economic or symbolic nature, or, indeed, if these roles can ever be fundamentally separated. Let's consider some possibilities. Some of the following suggestions are popular misconceptions, others are academic theories, while others are little more than educated guesses, but they all deserve some consideration.

Nit Combs?

It is clear that combs had a practical purpose. Primarily they were used for grooming, and in a shampoo-free world, they were no doubt important in physically cleaning hair; as much is suggested by Ibn Fadlan (Chapter 4). Another important use would have been the removal of lice. Attempts to identify invertebrates on the teeth of combs found in Britain and on the continent have been largely unsuccessful. However, some positive identifications have been made elsewhere in Europe, and in the Middle East different conditions of preservation and more robust methods of extraction have yielded significant quantities of head lice.[4] However, although head lice (*Pediculus humanus*) are frequently found in environmental samples from Viking-Age towns, the absence of evidence for their presence on Viking-Age combs from York may be a clue as to their utility. Combs with very fine teeth, suitable for the removal of lice, are not common in Viking Age Britain; the single-sided composite types that were most common were probably too coarse for this job.[5] Moreover, double-sided combs from this period frequently fail to follow the Roman precedent for the type: one set of coarse teeth, and one set of fine teeth. Rather, early medieval double-sided combs are generally characterised by two sets of teeth of broadly the same gauge. Thus, Viking-Age combs were for grooming; they were more concerned with the display of 'good-looking' hair, than they were with the maintenance of a healthy head (at least in the way we understand health).

Beard Combs?

A number of small, fine-toothed combs recovered from excavations of brochs and other Iron-Age sites in Scotland have been posited as beard combs (fig. 16).[6] Unfortunately, techniques for the analysis and interpretation of toothwear are not yet sufficiently developed to be of utility in the identification of the vagaries of use, and as yet there is no firm evidence to support this supposed function. Moreover, similar combs are not known from the Viking Age. If Viking men used special, miniature combs to groom their beards, we have yet to find any. We can probably assume that most composite combs were intended for use on the head.

Whatever their precise practical purpose, it may be that combs had an additional, less prosaic function. As a straightforward item of utility devoid of meaning, the method of production is time-inefficient, and decoration seems excessive. Thus, it does not seem eccentric to propose some form of symbolic purpose for these objects. In order to establish what this purpose might have been, it is necessary to consider the documentary and literary record.

16. A Pre-Viking miniature 'beard' comb. (Drawing Hayley Saul, courtesy Trustees of National Museums Scotland)

Liturgical Combs?

Given the contexts in which most early medieval scholarship was undertaken, it is not surprising to discover that the most useful contemporary references to combs come from ecclesiastical sources. In particular, the text at the head of this chapter is of interest. This is taken from a letter from Alcuin (once again) to Riculf, Archbishop of Mainz, and, together with an associated riddle, is suggestive of an apparently inordinate period of time spent ruminating upon the nature of a particular comb, given as a gift.

However, it is unlikely that this letter refers to a 'standard production' comb. Much more likely is what has become known as a liturgical comb. Such combs could be extremely ornate and very large, and were often carved from ivory. Their use is not clear, but they may have been part of the paraphernalia of the liturgy.

An early example of such a comb is known from the tomb of St Cuthbert, now housed at the Treasury in Durham Cathedral (fig. 17).[7] On first appearances, Cuthbert's comb seems to be of surprisingly rough craftsmanship (particularly in relation to the elaborately embroidered silks and textiles from the same context, and the finely carved coffin itself), but its size and lavish use of raw material (elephant ivory) are remarkable.[8] It has been suggested that it was designed and constructed through the repeated use of a predetermined unit of measurement, with reference to the 'golden mean', but suggestions that its rough, undecorated appearance relate to the fact that it is of early medieval date are unfounded, as this book attests.

Similar large, double-sided combs cut from a single piece of ivory are known from European contexts throughout the Middle Ages. The received wisdom is that many such combs (especially the highly ornate examples) are *liturgical* in function. Indeed, it is notable that during the post-Conquest period, repeated calls were made to the clergy to keep their hair tidy and beards shaved,[9] while it has been suggested that in the high medieval Church, a symbolic connection existed between the combing of the hair and tidying of the mind in preparation for the receipt of mass. Moreover, the combing of the celebrant's hair may even have played an important part in the liturgy itself, and it may be significant that thirteenth-century documents (and their successors through to the twentieth century) prescribe the use of an ivory comb after the anointing of a bishop during consecration. This ceremony probably has ties to the anointing of kings (see above).

Such a connection may be more applicable to later examples than those of the eleventh century, and there is a lack of documentary evidence for the liturgical use of combs prior to the thirteenth century.[10] However, St

Cuthbert's example (which, notably, shows signs of use-wear), together with the documentary references preserved in the writings of Alcuin, and the fact that Bede also mentions the use of gold and ivory combs as items of gift exchange,[11] suggest that at the very least combs had some currency among high-status groups in the early Middle Ages, including the high clergy. In detail, it has been suggested that certain aspects of Alcuin's writing indicate a comb with particular formal similarities to the

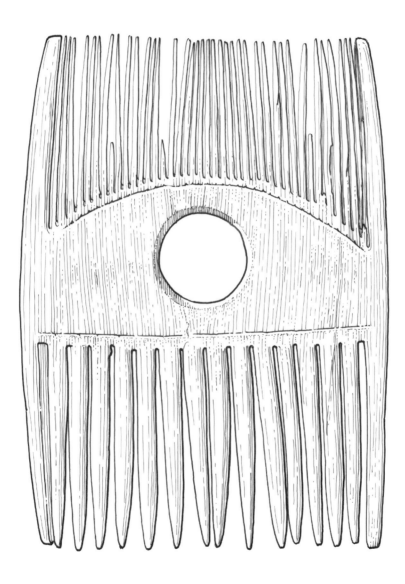

17. St Cuthbert's comb. (Drawing by Nick Griffiths)

St Cuthbert example.[12] Whatever, the extravagance of design evident in such combs suggests that they performed some symbolic or ornamental role in the Middle Ages, if not before.[13] Arguable support comes from the excavation of the graves of putative priests at Ripon Cathedral.[14] However, the combs concerned have the appearance of 'ordinary' composite combs, rather than large or ornate, one-piece liturgical types, and even if we accept these as examples of ecclesiastical equipment, it contributes little to the attempt to explain their role.

Combs as Symbols?

Moving away from combs as art, we turn now to their representation *in* the visual arts, as this may give us some indication as to their social relevance. Combs are not frequent motifs in Viking-Age art, which is generally populated by mythical animals, heroic figures and abstract designs, but we don't have to travel far in time in order to find very clear representations of grooming. The well-known Merovingian mortuary stone from Niederdollendorf, attests to the significance of hair combing in the early medieval period (see fig. 13, above),[15] as does early Irish sculpture featuring a striking 'hair-dressing' scene at Clonmacnoise in Co. Offaly (fig. 18). Moreover, the Pictish sculpture from Orkney's Brough of Birsay (fig. 19) uses hairstyle as part of a visual code of hierarchy. This is significant; even if artistically heightened, the idea of a leader styling their hair in a manner different to that of their followers must have been understood by the artist's audience. Moreover, combs themselves are very frequently depicted on Pictish symbol stones.[16] It has been suggested that they relate to women, though the evidence for this association is tenuous at best.[17] It has also been postulated that most of the recognised Pictish symbols relate to personal names, and that the mirror and comb motifs are an addendum meaning something along the lines of 'to the spirits of the departed', although the precise link between the symbol and the symbolised is unclear. Whatever the meaning, the use of combs as a sculptural motif suggests that there *was* some significance beyond simple hygienic function. Few doubt the significance of mirrors in prehistoric society,[18] and their association with combs is thus evocative.

The Lives of Combs

These snippets of information from text and sculpture are invaluable, but the bulk of data that we may use in order to understand comb use

18. Hair behaviour in sculpture, Clonmacnoise, Ireland. (Image by David Petts)

19. Hair and status in sculpture: the Brough of Birsay, Orkney. (Drawing by Steve Ashby)

comes from the archaeological contexts of the finds themselves. It is to the combs and their contexts that we now turn, as we begin to construct comb *biographies*, in which we consider the various arenas in which they operated, along with the people with whom and things with which they interacted over their lifetimes. We will consider combs as items of personal and social display, as agents of power, and as functioning tools. But first we must consider their role as gifts.

Combs to Give and to Receive

Let's think back, and reflect on what we've learnt so far. Combs cannot have been inexpensive or disposable items, given that the construction process was long and protracted, that the range of materials perceived to be appropriate was limited (to the extent that it was occasionally necessary to import materials from distance) and that repair seems to have been seen as worthwhile, at least in some cases. This realisation led us to the question of how these objects were distributed. Were they major

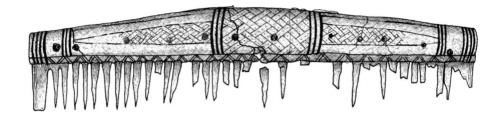

20. A so-called 'horse comb' from Viking-Age Sweden. (Drawing by Hayley Saul)

items of gift exchange? There are a number of indications that, at least in some contexts, they could be. A rare bronze comb of Anglian date was found at Whitby,[19] and this has a close parallel from Puy-de-Dôme, in the Massif Central, France.[20] Such a separation must surely relate to the circulation of a limited number of ornate combs as diplomatic gifts. There is also a fragment of a silver comb in the Cuerdale hoard, and a probably more complete example from the early medieval silver hoard discovered at the Broch of Burgar, Orkney (though reported and briefly described by George Petrie in the nineteenth century, this comb is now lost).[21] Thus, it seems likely that a certain number of combs were produced in metals, and this might support the hypothesis that they had a role in reciprocal gift exchange among the aristocracy. Such a mechanism was no doubt equally important in the distribution of bone, antler and ivory combs, particularly highly ornate, or impractically large 'monumental' examples (fig. 20), but conceivably also in the acquisition of a much larger subset of combs, particularly in the ninth century. The extent and scale of any such circulation can only be speculated upon.

Magic Combs?

When it comes to comb use, with the weight of ethnographic analogy, as well as documentary and literary evidence, behind us, there is certainly scope for consideration of their having some meaning or use beyond basic hygienic function. Indeed, some combs cry out to be interpreted in imaginative ways. For example, a number of distinctive handled combs featured a hollow chamber in the handle.[22] It has been speculated that these were designed for the secretion of some object or substance (perhaps a relic or charm; in this respect the twelfth-century *Song of Roland*'s reference to the curation of the relics of St Denis in the hilt of an ostentatious sword is of note),[23] and the presence of perforations in many examples suggests that perhaps fragrant herbs were inserted there. This may have been solely related to their aromatic nature, but may also have had a magical or apotropaic significance; in all likelihood the two could not be separated.[24] It is worth remembering that throughout history and prehistory, special qualities have been associated with antler, as a material taken from the deer. The perceived properties of the material have included magical valency and protective powers, as well as its influence upon fertility. It is perfectly reasonable to suppose that combs may have had such an amuletic function, at least in some contexts.

Display Combs?

These material significances are important, but I think it would be wrong to focus too much on them; that would be to undersell the work of the combmaker. We are not, after all, talking about unworked pieces of antler, but highly crafted – and frequently ornamented – personal items. Neither are they purely decorative pieces, but rather socially charged objects with a nonetheless important practical function. Numerous early medieval composite combs have been found throughout England, Scotland, Scandinavia and Frisia (now the Low Countries and the area close to the German Bight). Given this frequency, they represent a considerable, and thus far underexploited, resource for the understanding of ethnicity and culture. The occurrence of suspension holes on many combs might suggest that they were worn as something of a dress accessory, perhaps suspended from the belt by a thong. Certain combs frequently use what has come to be referred to as a 'display side convention', while other, small combs were equipped with ornate cases (fig. 21). All of these phenomena might be taken to indicate the importance of combs in display, and such a mode of use goes some way towards explaining their elaborate construction and decoration. Moreover, it makes the idea of their use in the expression and structuring of identity even more appealing.

The situation is a little more complex than this, however, as a large number of combs display no evidence that they could have been either suspended or held in a case. Moreover, many were clearly too large to be carried in this way. Such combs nonetheless feature complex ornament; in the case of some early Viking-Age examples, more than is visible on the cased or suspended forms. These combs, then, were still intended to be read, but perhaps by a particular audience. If given as gifts, then the audience may have been either the receiver, or any watching crowd. In use, the comb may either have been displayed in the household, or brought out for grooming. It is possible, then, that it was only seen in the most intimate situations, when slaves, servants or perhaps family were required to groom the lord and lady of the house. Medieval literature provides some circumstantial support for grooming taking place in a particular intimate personal context. For instance, in *Kormák's Saga*, Kormák offers to comb the hair of Steingerd, the object of his affection.[25] This seems to be a particularly intimate exchange, and to grant someone permission to engage in such a personal activity implies some form of closeness. There are numerous other examples, and such references seem to prefigure the much later exchange of boxwood and ivory combs between lovers.[26] Of course, there is no direct link, and we should not assume continuity of meaning throughout the Middle Ages, but these examples do provide useful analogies, and remind us of the possibility that the combing of hair may have been a ritual that took place in particularly private, intimate or personally and socially charged situations.

Whether in use as items of public display, or for a much more restricted audience, what is key is that these objects were being used to make statements and signals, to communicate in particular ways in particular contexts. It is fundamental that we have an appreciation, if not a detailed understanding, of this.

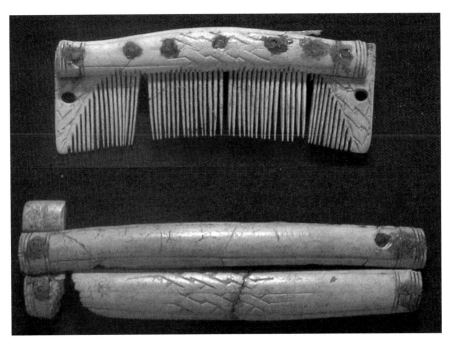

21. A well-made comb and case from a grave at Skaill Bay, Orkney. (Image by Steve Ashby, courtesy Trustees of the National Museums of Scotland)

Combs and Communication

But what were they communicating? Again, we can draw upon written evidence to help us here. Documentary and literary sources seem to support the idea that dress was an important signifier of identity.[27] Indeed, it may be that dress accessories, ornaments and other personal items were of particular significance in social expression, and we can learn something here from what we know about better-studied artefacts such as weaponry and, in particular, jewellery. One very important element of identity, and an element on which such dress and portable items may have had the power to act, is in the negotiation of social status. It is appropriate, then, before considering the particular role of combs in the communication of ideas about status, to take a look at dress and personal items more generally, and to consider their part in this noisy social discourse.

Throughout the early medieval period, the possession of fine dress accessories such as brooches was a clear mark of social, economic and political status. No doubt this phenomenon was borne out of a widely held appreciation of the roles played by particular objects in gift exchange, coupled with a power to restrict access to certain resources and types of objects. However, that does little to explain why particular *sorts* of objects are more closely implicated in this form of negotiation than others – the relationship between weapons and power may be rather self-evident; the rationale for the elevation of brooches to this forum of social competition is less so. It has been argued that the early medieval use of brooches actively refers back to a late Roman tradition, wherein such accoutrements constituted badges of office. The tradition persisted among the leaders of warbands in the decades that followed the Roman withdrawal from Britain, and thus their enduring relationship with structures of power was born.[28]

This is a convincing suggestion, but if this is the key reason for jewellery coming to play such an important role in social negotiation, then it does not provide a good analogy for combs, and we need to identify some alternative mechanism by which our object of choice found its social relevance. It seems most likely, then, that the role of combs in the production of status rather relates to the relationship between hair and elite identity that we discussed in Chapter 4. Combs constitute the equipment of a technology of social exclusion; they signify that their owners and wearers are members of the elite, as they are direct references to the ability to spend time and resources on personal display (itself an indicator of elite identity).

In later years, combs became available on the urban market, leading to something of a transformation in the types of social statement one was able to make with a comb. Their previous place at the table of the elite now made them symbols of aspiration, forcing the upper echelons of society to commission increasingly elaborate forms, or else to find new ways of expressing their status. In Orkney, the large number of late Viking and medieval combs no doubt relates to an expanding demographic able to acquire decorative dress accessories, and as such is testament to the economic wealth of the islands during this period.[29]

Recent work on these Orcadian combs suggested that they played a very particular role in the display of status and identity, acting as an important medium for symbolic messaging. It was argued that certain combs had links with a wealthy and powerful mercantile class, and that other variations in comb form were related to aspects of local or regional identity.[30] Whether or not one chooses to believe this particular argument, it is significant that comb manufacture is not evidenced in late Norse Orkney. Furthermore, it would have been difficult to produce combs here, given the lack of a native deer population to act as a raw material resource, and a lack of towns in which combmakers could work. The fact that there was a perceived need to import these objects from Scandinavia tells us just how central they were to identity and society in Norse Orkney.

The Orkney study shows us that while status is important, there are other facets of social identity that may be expressed through material culture: things like age, gender, ethnicity, kinship, group affiliation, religion or even personal identification. These might not always be equally important, and may be expressed differently in different contexts. By way of analogy, the abundance of small artefacts in late Iron-Age (pre-Viking) Scotland is notable, and it has been argued that the reason for this is an increased desire to express identity through the medium of portable material culture.[31]

Across Europe, few combs can be explicitly tied to individuals, though a number display runic inscriptions; there are, for example, several from Trondheim, and examples from Whitby (Yorks) and Nassington (Northants), while a comb from Aarhus in Denmark is marked with an English-name –HIKUIN (perhaps the comb's manufacturer?).[32] This comb's counterpoint is a case from Lincoln, which is inscribed with the message that 'Thorfastr made a good comb'.[33] These examples, together with historically referenced examples (such as the comb in St Cuthbert's tomb; see above) are of note, but it is possible that combs had a more general role in the construction of broader forms of identity.

Combs, Contexts, and the Ritual of the Everyday

The small variations in comb form and ornament will, as we will see, have been important in communicating social difference and identity. In general terms, however, we will find the significance of combs in their role in apparently mundane (but actually highly socially charged) activities such as grooming practice, or what we might call the 'ritual of the everyday'. Such practices were not unstructured, and the participants, audiences and contexts involved were no doubt culturally regulated.

So, how and where did this grooming take place? The documentary record is largely silent on this issue, but we can steal a few glimpses of context if we look hard enough. We might return to Ibn Fadlan's account of communal washing among the Rus, but medieval Nordic literature also contains a number of brief references to grooming rituals. For instance, in *Skaldskaparmal*, in the *Edda*, there are several mentions of the practice of hair-bleaching or washing.[34] These passages suggest that it was seen as undesirable to share the water used in this process with those of lower social standing. Thus, personal grooming might have been a public practice, but if so, it was not free of social rules, and the implied connection between cleanliness, grooming, and status is something that has a lot of resonance in our discussions so far.

Such structuring might have had implications for where the ritual itself may have taken place. Could grooming among the aristocracy, for instance, have taken place in particular buildings or arenas, closed off from public view? Could grooming of freemen have been assisted by architectures that allowed communal bathing, but which restricted access by social inferiors? Just as the Romans had bathhouses, perhaps the Nordic sauna provided a key locale. Saunas and bathhouses may have been present in the Finno-Ugric world before the Viking Age, but their existence and distribution is difficult to trace. They seem to have been known in Iceland by the thirteenth century (in *Erbyggja Saga*, the character known as Styrr builds a bathhouse in which he traps a group of berserkers),[35] but archaeologically, they are poorly evidenced, unless we suppose that this was one function of the ubiquitous 'sunken floor buildings'. It should be noted that most of the excavated rural settlement sites in Scandinavia are from Denmark and its environs, and though there is little clear evidence of bathhouses here, we might expect them to be more common further north. That said, there is little evidence even in the east of the Viking world, as at Staraja Ladoga, in Russia, for instance. In the British Isles, a bathhouse has been speculatively identified at the Brough of Birsay, in Orkney, where the proposed structure lies in close association with a high-status dwelling, perhaps the earl's residence.[36] There is little in the way of clear support for this idea, and either way, the absence of bathhouses from the well-excavated towns of Viking England and Scandinavia is notable. Nonetheless, it is a truism that saunas have always played host to an important ritual of cleansing and relaxation, but one which had particular health and religious implications, and simultaneously facilitated socialising within particular groups.[37] Perhaps combs were even seen as part of the toolkit of this social and magico-medical practice? It is difficult to do more than speculate, but we should at least consider the possibility that grooming may have taken place in social arenas to which access was carefully defined. In other situations one might assume grooming to be either a more private, intimate activity (as illustrated in saga and Celtic literature), or one performed in public, as a way of affirming group identity (as in Ibn Fadlan's account of Rus haircare). Either way, social context is significant to the act, and the sociological ideas about the technology of haircare discussed above are of much value.

In what follows, we will explore the particular facets of personal identity to which comb and grooming might contribute. We have shown that combs rose to general prominence through their role in grooming, as an item associated with the maintenance of elite identity. It thus follows that they became a medium for display, whereupon they developed as a canvas for the communication of more complex, more diverse, and more nuanced messages. The very act of owning a comb certainly made a big statement, but the choice of form and ornament articulated much more subtle narratives. It is these stories that we now turn to: what did the particular detail of a comb say about its owner? And how did the combs, and the stories they told, develop over the two and a half centuries of the Viking Age?

Communicating Through Combs: Identity

In very simple terms, and putting aside key issues such as kinship, allegiance or group membership (to which the early medievalist must repeatedly return), one might consider identity on the following dimensions: age, gender, status and ethnicity. The first of these two categories are difficult for the archaeologist to address in the abstract, and instead are the subject of discussion in Chapter 6, where we will discuss special contexts in which particular combs may be associated with individuals of known age or sex. These contexts are, of course, furnished graves. Interpretations of these burials may ultimately impact upon our understanding of age and gender-based identities in life, but in England in particular, where such mortuary evidence is rare, it is difficult to make clear statements about the use of combs in the construction of identities borne out of categorisation in terms of sexual distinctions or life stages. However, two facets of identity that are arguably a little more easy to access from settlement evidence are status and ethnicity. We discuss each below, but these areas have considerable overlap; one might expect that in certain cases the symbols of a particular ethnic group might develop to become representative of a certain level of social or economic status. In these situations, as we will see, the appropriation of such symbols in order to improve one's standing in society might be seen as emulation of a particular ethnic group. Members of the elite have always appropriated symbols and touchstones of diverse aspects of identity, incorporating them into the corpus of references they use to affirm their status, and we will see that this was the case with Viking-Age combs. First, however, in order to understand the precise means by which combs may have played a role in negotiating social boundaries, it is necessary to say a little about social structure, and the basis of power in the early medieval period.

Combs, Ethnicity and Status

There are many myths and misunderstandings about the structure of society in early medieval Europe. This is not the place to go over the subject in depth, but it suffices to say that old-fashioned ideas about the 'democracy' of Anglo-Saxon England may be some way off the mark. That is not to say that we are investigating an England identical to that seen after the Norman Conquest, but certainly the first seeds of feudalism had been sown long before 1066. We know that slave labour was central to the economy, but we don't know precisely what this entailed, or how it was organised. Indeed, it is precisely this insecurity, this regional variability, this pace of change that makes the Viking Age so interesting to study; in the space of a couple of centuries we see significant transformation of social structure, economy, landscape, religion, and identity. It is our task to make sense of all this.

Carried along on these currents, the nature of power and status changed considerably over the course of our period of interest, with social position at various times being more or less dependent on kinship relations, military might, economic wealth or ideological dominance. While social rank and economic standing could, theoretically, represent discrete phenomena in any given context, herein 'socioeconomic status' is employed as an all-embracing term.

But how was power expressed, or structured? For much of the early medieval period, people were bound into various relationships of obligation. The elite thus maintained a retinue, to which they would promise land, gifts or protection in return for service. In particular, the exchange of gifts was the glue that held early medieval society together. Gifts could be exchanged between parties of similar social standing (kings for instance, who may exchange gifts in order to demonstrate alliance, if not allegiance or fealty), or between a lord and members of his retinue (as seen in the classic image of the Viking feast, or the sharing out of plundered wealth). The exchange of gifts thus constituted a means of

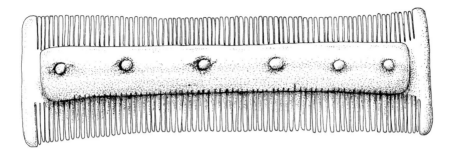

22. A double-sided comb typical of Anglo-Saxon England and 'Pictish' northern Scotland. (Drawing by Pat Walsh, Northamptonshire Archaeology)

23. An ornate 'hogbacked' comb from York, dating to the pre-Viking period. (Image by Steve Ashby, courtesy York Museums Trust)

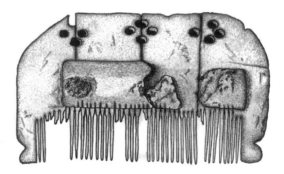

24. An ornate pre-Viking comb from Orkney, northern Scotland. (Image by Steve Ashby, courtesy National Museums Scotland)

consolidating political and military alliances, as well as acting as a more basic demonstration of mutual respect and understanding, and may even have led to the competitive gift-giving well evidenced in recent non-western societies. Through such mechanisms, it is easy to see how the items exchanged could themselves become tied up in the politics of status and power.[38] These items seem to have included hair combs, and it is likely that it is in the context of such exchange that combs maintained much of their social power.

Moreover, it was through such mechanisms that the elite were relieved of the duty of labour, meaning that they had more freedom to spend time and resources on items and activities that might otherwise appear frivolous or excessive. Such expenditure in itself came to be a marker of the elite, hence the appearance of elaborate brooches and other dress accessories. Might combs, or even a well-styled head of hair, be seen in a similar way? If so, combs might be seen as a particularly appropriate item to be exchanged between members of the elite, or to be presented to supporters as a demonstration of trust, thanks and protection. The exchange of such items no doubt had a complex grammar that is largely lost to us today, but it is clear that combs stood for *something*.

Combs, Power and Identity in the Early Viking Age

Clearly not all combs held the same meanings in all times and places; social context was important, as were the qualities of different forms of combs. In the British Isles, prior to the Scandinavian settlements, the simple, unornamented double-sided combs (fig. 22) that were a fixture of Anglo-Saxon settlements seem best characterised as a comb for everyday use. Nonetheless, not everyone would have had one, and they no doubt acted as one of many social indicators of being 'free', if not of higher status. In contrast, the highly ornate, often unique single-sided combs of both England (fig. 23) and Atlantic Scotland (fig. 24) must have been produced to commission, and were doubtless signifiers of aristocratic, even royal, status.

25. An ornate handled comb from York. (Drawing by Nick Griffiths)

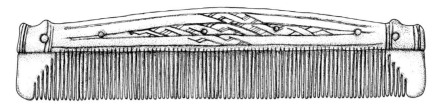

26. A large, early Viking comb from Birka, Sweden. (Drawing by Pat Walsh, Northamptonshire Archaeology)

Furthermore, they may have switched hands as part of diplomatic and reciprocal gift exchange (perhaps to consolidate alliances between ethnic and political groups in unstable times[39]). The fact that some examples, including the Birsay example (pictured in fig. 24), bear evidence of repair is telling, and such combs seem very unlikely to have had a purely functional, hygienic role. They certainly held some significance in Pictland, where their representation on sculpture is arguably suggestive of some political or cosmological association. Nonetheless, as we have seen, no comb was inert; they all sent out messages of some sort.

That their significance was maintained through gift exchange is not to say that it did not derive from their role in haircare; we have already seen that such practice is frequently meaningfully undertaken. Moreover, we know that personal appearance was an important signifier of status in early medieval Britain; dress accessories such as brooches were often ornate, even monumental, while, as we have seen, the depiction of a chieftain and his followers on the Brough of Birsay stone suggests that dress, and hairstyle in particular, could be used as badges of status (see fig. 19, above). As we have seen, in Scotland in particular, it has been suggested that there was, at some point in the first millennium AD, a switch from a community-centred, architecturally mediated identity, to a more personal, artefact-based self-image. If this is true, it seems likely that highly decorative combs, as one of the more commonly found artefacts of the period, played some part in such a system. They may even have been among the key drivers of such a change.

Other combs from this period, such as the highly distinctive 'handled' forms that we see in England between around AD 700 and 1100, vary widely in terms of quality (fig. 25). Nonetheless this form clearly represents a discrete group, with its very noticeable form and unusual style of decoration. As we have seen, these combs also seem to have been used in distinctive ways; some examples contained hollow cavities in the handle, intended perhaps for the secretion of aromatic herbs or amulets. Does this suggest something very particular about the ownership or function of these combs? In addition, combing your hair with a handled comb, as opposed to a non-handled form, requires holding the comb in a different position, resulting in a subtly different action. We might thus expect such combs to have marked out their owners as a distinct – perhaps alien – group. It has been suggested that these items relate to Frisians, or at least that they originally did, before being taken up by England's Anglo-Saxon population. However we interpret them, they certainly served some messaging purpose, whether this related more closely to status, ethnicity or job description. It is notable that they persist right through the Middle Saxon period and the era of Scandinavian settlement, and thus clearly relate to a group with a prolonged presence or influence in England (see below).

The appearance of Scandinavians in the British Isles brought with it large, ornate combs of a style that had been developing in northern Europe for the last century or so (fig. 26). These combs thus had a well-understood grammar; people recognised the form and ornament, and knew what it meant to have one – again they were no doubt produced to commission by magnates, and circulated by a system of gift exchange. Scandinavians knew how to *read* these combs. They clearly had the capacity to invoke or enhance status, and a number of particularly well-made, ostentatious examples are known from sites such as Birka in Sweden; here very large, ornate 'horse' combs (see fig. 20, above) are of particular note. Such combs are impractical as either dress accessories or toilet implements, but their coarse teeth *are* paralleled in modern horse combs, so their attribution to a role in equine grooming may be well placed. If so, it is interesting that they bear such close comparison with 'human' combs; they are larger, more elaborate variations on the theme, which perhaps tells us something about relationships between the ninth-century Scandinavian aristocracy and their horses. Either way, they are certainly best interpreted as a form of symbolic medium, a sort of 'monumental' comb. The same may even be true of much less accomplished manufactures; these no doubt represent imitations, manufactured in order to help fulfil certain social aspirations. They thus anticipate a trend that was, as we will see, to pick up considerable pace in the tenth and eleventh centuries.

Interestingly, neither the human nor equine variants of this comb form ever took off as products to be manufactured in Britain and Ireland, where the ninth century saw the continuing production and use of native forms, though their significance to Scandinavians was not lost even after they drifted out of fashion. We can see this, as a number were curated as heirlooms, or reworked into pendants.

Combs, Power and Identity in the Later Viking Age

The tenth and eleventh centuries were a time of great social and economic change, and combs were not immune to such currents, as the growth of towns and the movement to a more commercial economy created new opportunities for producers and consumers alike. It is therefore worth us looking at some of the changes in comb fashions and forms over this time period, as they may well tell us something about the changing role of the comb in this new, emerging world.

With the development of the urban marketplace, combmakers began to produce their wares on a larger scale, arguably taking less care in manufacture and ornament, but opening the market up to aspiring town-dwellers, who were now able to acquire new forms of objects that were previously available only to the elite (fig. 27). This seems to have been the case in Scandinavia, northern continental Europe, England and Ireland alike (manufacturing sites in Scotland remain oddly elusive). In the tenth century, England, Ireland and parts of Denmark started to see the appearance of combs that were much less uniform in morphology, their profiles apparently being dictated by the natural curve of a red deer's antler (fig. 28). They thus vary considerably in form, but are rarely manufactured or decorated to high standards. They are rarely evenly profiled, and ornament could be rudimentary, idiosyncratic, asymmetrical or even absent. Many such combs lacked suspension holes, and if carried on the person, they must have been kept in pouches of some sort, so that their form was only revealed in private, grooming contexts. Interestingly, by the eleventh century many were being decorated with chevron or chequerboard ornament – just the kind of motifs that began to appear in Romanesque architecture around this time. Were combmakers and stonemasons speaking a common symbolic language?

In tenth- to twelfth-century England, Ireland and, it seems, northern France (perhaps anticipating the approaching political unity with England),

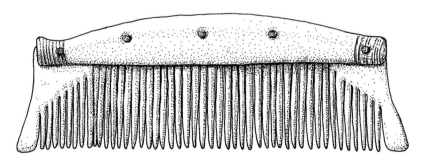

27. A late Viking-Age comb from Denmark. (Drawing by Pat Walsh, Northamptonshire Archaeology)

28. An irregular, late Viking-Age comb from York. (Drawing by Hayley Saul)

the most affordable combs were certainly produced in cattle horn, with a simple bone connecting plate. Such combs were produced to a very clear template and have consistent dimensions, but were crudely manufactured, and seem to have been wholly lacking in artistic content. They are rarely preserved in their entirety, but some examples are known.

Interestingly, such combs were not produced in Scandinavia, but the region did experience the production of new forms, again to a set template (see figs 21, 27, above). These combs had a much more functional appearance than their predecessors, but the use of elaborate cases (which must certainly have doubled the combmaker's investment in time and energy, and as such were probably relatively costly) tell another story. Though the tenth-century fashion was for smaller, less ostentatious combs, most examples were nonetheless well made, and they continued to be used in graves in areas where pagan burial persisted until this late date. Even as they fell out of use in gift exchange, these combs were certainly still intended to make a visual statement as a dress accessory. In Norway, the demand was considerable; large quantities of reindeer antler were shipped from the herds of the Hardangervidda plateau for use in comb manufacture in Bergen, but such was the desire for this material that it was also exported hundreds of kilometres to towns now in Sweden.[40]

Throughout northern Europe – with the exception of England – this move to large-scale production for commercial output saw its apotheosis between the late Viking Age and the end of the Middle Ages, where a range of ornate forms were produced using complex arrangements of copper-alloy rivets and plating as ornament. Quite why this trend was never experienced in the southern British Isles no doubt has its basis in the different roles played by combs in identity construction and communication in different socio-political contexts. Comb styles in England were now set on a different trajectory to that of Scandinavia; in the former we may perceive a trend towards simple, utilitarian combs (fig. 29), ultimately culminating in the disposable 'nit combs' of the late Middle Ages, while in the latter composite combs continue to play an important role in personal display even into the fifteenth century. Thus, though in the Viking Age combs seem to have played similar social roles across the Viking world, by the eleventh century things were starting to change, and the medieval trajectories of the various parts of northern Europe began to diverge. We couldn't hope for clearer evidence of a connection between politics, social structure and the ways in which combs were used. Composite combs continued to thrive in Scandinavia and its colonies, while in England, under new Norman management, they died. The deaths of combs, as individual items, are the subject of our next chapter.

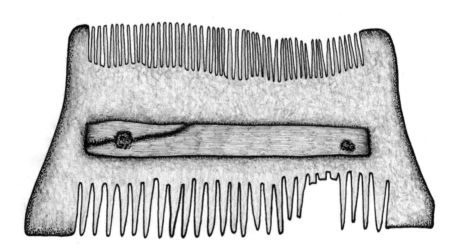

29. Combs of bone and horn. (Image by Steve Ashby; Drawing by Hayley Saul)

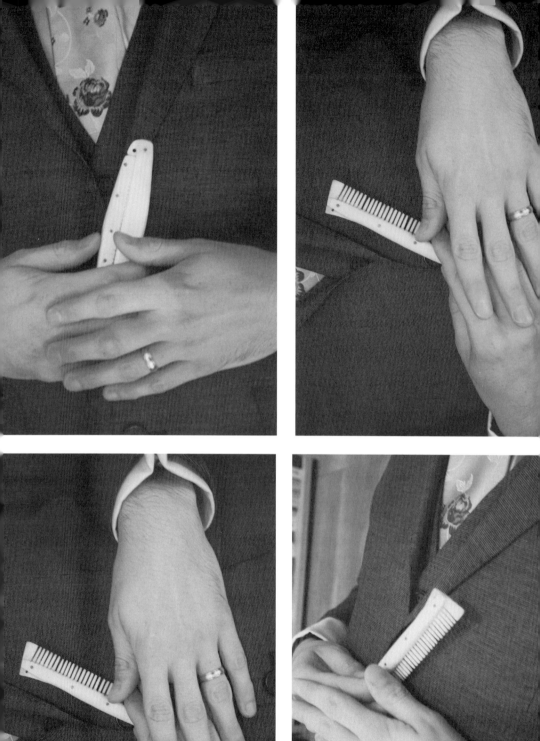

6

Ends

Then she steered her ship up Hvammsfjord and came to a certain ness, and stayed there a little while. There Unn lost her comb, so it was afterwards called Kambsnes.

Laxdaela Saga, Chapter V[1]

Likewise in the links of Tranabie, in Westra, have been found graves in the sand ... in one of which was seen a man lying with his sword on the one hand, and a Daneish ax on the other, and others that have had dogs, and combs and knives buried with them, which seems to be an instance of the way how the Danes (when they were in this country) buried their dead.

James Wallace, 1693[2]

The winds of the North Atlantic can be ferocious. By the 1980s and early 1990s, coastal erosion on the Orcadian isle of Sanday had begun to reveal the remains of a Viking-Age boat burial and, as is so often the case, threatened to follow revelation with destruction.[3] Thanks to the quick work of a team of archaeologists battling storm and tide, the site was excavated and recorded before it could be lost. The find turned out to be one of the most significant Scotland had seen for decades.[4]

Following the discovery of human bones, and finds including iron nails and lead weights, rescue excavations recovered the remains of a small, but complex, boat burial. Despite the difficult conditions, it was recorded with enough precision for us to be able to reconstruct a little of the ritual of burial. A boat (about 7 metres long, and built in the Scandinavian tradition somewhere outside Orkney) was lowered into a specially dug pit, and sealed with loose stones at either end, while one end of the boat itself was filled up with rocks, leaving the remainder as something of a burial chamber. Within this chamber, three people were buried – a young man, an elderly woman and a child – in what we may imagine as a moment of considerable meaning, emotion and ritual.

These individuals (who may or may not have been part of the same family) were surrounded by objects, some of which may have belonged to them in life, and some of which were clearly heirlooms of some kind. The man had a sword, a set of arrows and perhaps a shield, as well as a bag of gaming pieces, a comb and some lead weights. At the feet of the old woman was placed an ornate (and now iconic) whalebone plaque, often thought of as playing a role in linen smoothing, but which clearly also had important status associations. Alongside the female burial were laid an array of textile tools, a sickle, a single brooch and a comb. The child appears to have been unaccompanied, though it should be said that there may have been other artefacts, as many would have been lost to erosion prior to excavation.[5]

We must realise that the moment of interment was probably not the end of people's engagement with the grave; the process of remembering would have continued long afterwards. However, the moment of burial is important in itself. The construction of the tableau was important, it would have been intended to be seen and experienced.[6] Who decided on what objects went into each burial, and how did they agree on what would be appropriate? How was the correct position in the grave established? There must have been norms and rules that were followed, but as to their nature and rationale, we can only speculate. Nonetheless, within this complex performance, there are elements about which we may be able to say a little. For instance, it may be possible to gain some understanding of the rationale behind the interment of particular types of object should we pay close attention to the life histories, the biographies, of such objects. How were brooches made, how were they traded, who gave, received, owned or wore them? How were they valued? In what contexts might they have changed hands – weddings? Births? Deaths? Were they disposed of when unfashionable, or curated as heirlooms, passed on from generation to generation? Was broken jewellery repaired, or simply thrown away? An understanding of these complex histories of human–object relationships, using archaeology, history, literature, art history and anthropology, can really give us a window onto the possible roles played by such objects in burial practice. What might otherwise seem like an impossibly complex and alien process suddenly becomes comprehensible, at least in part.

And of course, this is precisely what we have been doing for the hair comb. Armed with the knowledge of the foregoing pages, we can start to think about why combs played a part in the burials at Scar, and perhaps in mortuary ritual more generally. But let's begin with Scar.

Clasped between the hands of the male skeleton were the remains of a large antler comb. It is badly preserved, but enough remains for us to be confident that this was a large, well-manufactured, ornate comb, dating to the ninth or earliest tenth century – the sort of over-engineered object that first suggested to me that combs and hair may have had some form of elevated significance in the Viking world. These combs were never made in the British Isles, and it seems most likely that this example reached Orkney as a personal possession, perhaps of the man buried in the grave. Was it given to him to symbolise a relationship, perhaps between himself and a spouse or kinsman, a lord or tenant, an adversary or an ally? Either way, it may well have represented a little piece of home, an object familiar back in Scandinavia, and thus acquired a particular significance here, in the alien environment of northern Scotland, as a Norse colony was established. That such an object *was* significant is beyond dispute; it was one of a relatively restricted suite of objects added to the grave at Scar. This may suggest that it was important for the dead man to take a comb into the next life, but it also implies that the living found it useful as a kind of mnemonic device: a material reminder, used to help in the practice of remembering the dead.[7] Moreover, while gaming pieces, weapons and other items were important enough to be interred, only one item was held in the hands of the deceased, and this privilege goes to the comb. Why might this be? Was it placed there before, at, or after the moment of death? Is it representative of a moment of symbolic grooming or change? We have seen how grooming was an important practice in preparing and manipulating one's appearance in life, and that different hair-and-dress strategies were applied according to social context. Could this be representative of the ultimate bodily cleansing or transformation, as the deceased moves between the world of the living and that of the dead?

The treatment of the man's comb is remarkable enough, but what is even more interesting is that the elderly female in the grave was also interred with a comb. This was not held between her hands, but rather positioned alongside her, with a collection of other artefacts deliberately placed into the grave as goods. In this case, as for the man, the comb cannot be considered a dress accessory; rather it was deliberately added to the grave to play a particular role, or to make a particular statement. The old woman's other accoutrements sing of privilege and status, and like the man's, her comb was too large to be of use purely as a functional implement, but must have had status, or perhaps gift-giving associations. Its decoration is of a type not commonly encountered in Scotland, and probably dates it to the early or middle ninth century. Thus, like the brooch and whalebone plaque, the comb may suggest that the old woman was one of Orkney's first settlers, if it belonged to her and was brought by her to Orkney. However, it is interesting to note the lack of evidence for wear on the teeth of these combs (particularly the man's comb); if they were used at all, this was done very sparingly. Given the period of time for which they must have been kept, we might ask whether they were cherished gifts, a symbol of some form of relationship – perhaps even a marriage. Had they been held onto as a symbol of such a relationship in life, curated as 'best' combs, brought out only for special occasions, and disposed of when no longer relevant?

In contrast to the range of goods accompanying the adult burials, it is notable also that the child burial had no associated objects. Just as it may have been thought inappropriate to bury a child with weapons (though see Balnakeil, below), or with the trappings of wealth or occupations (such as gaming pieces or weaving equipment), so it was equally inappropriate to bury them with a comb. Why might this have been? Were combs acquired at a certain stage in life? Could they have materialised relationships between master and servant, or, perhaps, as we have suggested above, man and wife? Whatever, they said something, and their absence in this context may be as notable as their presence elsewhere in the burial.

A number of questions are obviously raised by this startling find. Why was one comb placed between the man's hands? Why was at least one of the combs apparently curated as an heirloom, and what changed to make it suddenly appropriate to take it out of the system altogether and inter it a grave? Why were combs put into the grave at all? As we will see, this was not an uncommon occurrence; there are, for example, hundreds of inhumation and cremation graves containing combs in the cemeteries near Birka, central Sweden. But why was this the case? Answers are not easily forthcoming, but by considering the situation a little more broadly, we may find some solutions. A broad tradition of comb interment may be traced back much further than this, and it serves us well to consider the particularities of this rite in various spatio-temporal contexts.

Comb Burial in Pre-Viking Britain

In the Anglo-Saxon cremation burials of the fifth and sixth centuries, combs often seem to be placed unburnt in the grave, together with the cremated remains, while some such burials contain very small, often crudely constructed combs.[8] Their teeth are often poorly cut, or even just 'suggested' by surface grooves. This surely suggests a symbolic or ornamental – rather than practical – role.

All this has led some to propose a special meaning for combs and grooming items in Anglo-Saxon England, as objects fundamentally associated with the construction and reformation of personal identity.[9]

With this in mind, a reference to the combing of the hair of the dead, again in the *Saga of the People of Laxardal*,[10] is notable, though this is of course from a later, and arguably spurious, context. The idea of grooming the dead is of course an enduring one; combs, for instance, play an important role in dressing the body in traditional Jewish mortuary ritual.

However, many Anglo-Saxon combs seem to have been broken prior to interment, perhaps suggesting a ritual 'killing' of the comb.[11] Such an act might be necessary if the comb – through its connection with the hair – was seen as being bound up with the identity of the deceased, and thus potentially exploitable in some spiritual way. Alternatively, combs may have been interred because of what they could *do* for the dead; perhaps they helped to ease the movement between life and death, playing a symbolic or magical role in bodily transformation, imitating their function for the living.[12]

Such a role might explain why combs were placed into the urn as a final stage in the funerary ritual, rather than being burnt with the body and other accompaniments, though this might equally be explained as an effort to prevent the comb being stolen from the pyre before it was completely destroyed. Whatever the precise meaning of the practice, it is clear that some – probably eschatological – reasoning led to the comb receiving an elevated emphasis in funerary ritual.

Comb Burial in Pre-Viking and Viking-Age Scandinavia

Combs are much less common in Anglo-Saxon inhumation contexts than cremations, but in Viking-Age inhumations they *are* relatively well known.[13] In these contexts, they are associated with a range of objects, including weaponry, jewellery and other domestic items.[14] In Scandinavia, the diversity of mortuary ritual is incredible, with combs being found in both cremations and inhumations in the large cemeteries around the cosmopolitan trading settlement of Birka, Sweden. Similar diversity is visible in Gotland, while a number of pre-Viking graves in Norway contain both hunting weapons and tools associated with handicraft, and have thus been proposed as belonging to hunter-combmakers. Back at Birka, an elaborate male grave of the Vendel (pre-Viking) period was furnished not only with weaponry, and with the body of a probably sacrificed slave, but also with a large elk antler behind the head.[15] The interred individual (known informally as the Elk Man) was clearly a man of some power and significance, but the meaning of the antler is unclear. Perhaps it indicates a role in some otherworldly, animist activity, or something more practical. Could he have been a shaman, a hunter, or perhaps even a combmaker? His role in life will remain a mystery to us, but in death someone clearly thought that he should be remembered with antler, suggesting some form of association with the material itself, or with the animals from whence it came.

Comb Burial in Viking-Age Britain

The roles played by combs in rituals of burial are not only elusive, but must also have been diverse. It is thus instructive to consider a few key examples of Viking-Age graves from the British Isles, and the evidence that combs played an important part in the ceremonial activities that took place there (fig. 30).

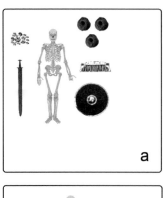

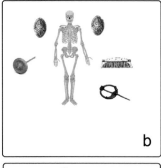

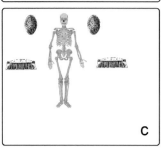

30. Schematic representations of burials from Scotland: (a) Balnakeil; (b) Westness; (c) Pierowall. (Drawn by Steve Ashby)

The Making of a Man? The Balnakeil Grave

At Balnakeil, Sutherland, in the north of the Scottish mainland, an unusual burial has been discovered.[16] This is the grave of a young (probably pre-teen) male, but whereas the child from Scar was accompanied by no grave goods, the Balnakeil boy experienced a lavishly equipped burial, complete with oversized sword, spear, shield, gaming pieces, fishing equipment and comb. Of course, we don't know if these objects ever really belonged to the boy in life, while the comb in particular is poorly preserved, and we await full publication of the grave, so it is difficult to speculate too much at present.

Nonetheless, the comb is clearly of the large, ornate, ninth- to tenth-century form that we have become used to seeing in Scotland's Viking-Age graves, and its inclusion no doubt makes a similar statement as does the associated weaponry; although just a child, this was no ordinary individual (we can assume as much from the skeleton itself, which shows unusual pathologies), and in death the community he left behind recreated his identity as that of a warrior or leader of some standing. Such was the transformative power of a few well-chosen objects.

A Woman of the World?
Cosmopolitan Female Burial at Westness, Orkney.

On the Orcadian island of Rousay, excavations between 1968 and 1984 revealed a Viking-Age settlement and burial complex, incorporating one of a small number of early medieval cemeteries in Orkney.[17] The cemetery contained over thirty graves, and stretched back to the pre-Viking period, with a number of Pictish Christian burials being followed by pagan Norse inhumations, including boat graves and those with boat-shaped settings. Two of those of the latter type compare at least superficially with the male and female burials at Scar, containing similar ranges of artefacts, including large, ornate combs. However, perhaps the most notable of all the graves was the first to be studied: the inhumation of a high-status woman and baby, probably fatalities of childbirth. The grave contained a large number of goods, many of a high quality. These included a number of tools related to textile manufacture (a craft very closely associated with women), as well as a pair of oval brooches and a collection of glass beads that no doubt hung over the chest like a necklace between them. This is fairly typical for a high-status female burial, but more unusual is a further range of metalwork, including a copper-alloy vessel, two Anglo-Saxon strapends and a very high-end penannular brooch in the Irish style. The collection truly points to a cosmopolitan woman (or community) with links around the British Isles as well as Scandinavia. Her comb, on the other hand, is of the type seen at Scar, and points back across the North Sea, where it is common in Scandinavia and the Low Countries. Even if Anglo-Saxon and Celtic metalwork made important statements in the burial of this unfortunate woman of privilege, her comb, which probably harks back to the Scandinavian homelands, seems to have acted as a key piece of mnemonic equipment.

Bracing Themselves for the Afterlife: Female Burial at the Pierowall Cemetery

Nineteenth-century excavations in the dunes behind Pierowall Bay on Westray, Orkney, uncovered what must have been a significant Viking-Age pagan cemetery. Unfortunately, a lack of clarity in the early records led to considerable confusion as to the topography and organisation of the cemetery, and prior to a thorough reanalysis of the material in the 1960s[18] it was impossible to associate finds with skeletons and grave architecture. Though there is still some ambiguity, some patterning is apparent. Among the seventeen or so graves, we might note a male individual laid out with something of a headstone, and accompanied by a spear, sword, shield and comb: clearly a high-status lordly or 'warrior' burial (Grave 1). Also of note was Grave 4, which contained the remains of a female buried wearing a string of beads with paired oval brooches, as well as a ringed pin and another brooch. Most interestingly, the grave also included *two* combs, apparently carefully positioned above the elbow of the woman's right arm. Graves 12 and 14 are also interesting, in that the female individuals enclosed therein not only wore pairs of oval brooches, but were also accompanied by pairs of combs. In Grave 12, they were riveted with copper alloy and held in cases, suggesting a relatively late (tenth-century or later) date and positioned on each shoulder. Multiple combs are fairly rare in the Viking-Age burials of the British Isles, but are not unknown in Scandinavia; for instance, 10 per cent of the comb-laden graves in Birka's cemeteries contained more than one comb.[19] Whether or not the individuals owned both the combs they were buried with is impossible to ascertain, but the occurrence of this pattern on three occasions at Pierowall is perhaps indicative of a local particularity in burial rites. We know that there was much variability in burial practice across the Viking world,[20] and it seems that the community at Pierowall found a particular role for pairs of combs in the burial of important women.

The Case of the Furnished Cist:
A Burial at Skaill Bay, Orkney

The antiquarian find of a cist (stone-lined box-burial) at Skaill Bay in Sandwick, Orkney, is of note in that it represents a grave type not commonly recognised in Viking-Age Scotland.[21] Associated animal bones suggest that it may have been cut into a settlement mound or midden; though it seems strange to us, in the past people could be buried in rubbish heaps with some ritual, and without negative implications. The grave contained a spear and possible arrowhead, a knife and whetstone and a small but well-made comb, together with a matching antler case (see fig. 21, above). Such cases only appear to be found in the graves of men; women probably carried their combs in pouches. In the past this grave had been claimed as one of Orkney's older graves, dating back at least to the early ninth century, but on the grounds of the comb and case such a date is unsupportable. This form is relatively rare in both Norway and northern Scotland, but emerges in southern and eastern Scandinavia no earlier than the start of the tenth century. Allowing time for the comb to reach Orkney, this must date to the first half of the tenth century, and is thus probably among the later pagan burials in Scotland. Moreover, it is suggestive of contacts with Denmark or the Low Countries – links not frequently stressed in Viking Scotland, which is often seen as being colonised from the area that is now Norway. It is important to realise that Scandinavia (and what are now Denmark, Norway and Sweden) were not in any way coherent at this point, and in its own way, the Skaill Bay comb and case are just as indicative of cosmopolitan contacts as is the Westness brooch.

Getting a Handle on Viking Burial:
The Cambois Cemetery

A slightly different form of Viking-Age burial is known from Cambois, Bedlington, in Northumberland, a region in which evidence of Scandinavian activity is surprisingly thin on the ground.[22] Here, three individuals (a young man and a middle-aged man and woman) were buried in a cist beneath a mound, with very few grave goods: simply a disc brooch and a comb. Parallels for both objects suggest deposition in the ninth or early tenth century.

The architecture of the grave is clearly not typical of Christian burial, but the absence of weapons is striking, and has led some to suggest that these represented Viking landowners, rather than any sort of warrior elite. Whether any such distinction can be made is unclear, and there may be another way to interpret the burial. The brooch is enamelled, and features elaborate animal designs, reflecting English or continental European practice, rather than anything paralleled in Scandinavia. Similarly, it is notable that the comb is of the handled type, much more well known in Anglo-Saxon England and Frisia than in Scandinavia. Perhaps this represents a Scandinavian elite attempting to adapt to the local social and political environment; they had given up their Scandinavian styles of dress, but held on to mound burial. Or was this even a local Northumbrian adoption of the Scandinavian tradition of mound burial? Either way, it is interesting to note that of only two objects interred in the grave, one was a comb. Even if they were both interpreted as dress accessories, their inclusion was clearly deliberate, so conspicuous are both items.

A Burning Issue: The Hesket-in-the-Forest Burial

A grave in Cumbria, at a place known as Hesket-in-the-Forest, provides our final case study.[23] Here, antiquarians discovered an unusual mound burial. Under the mound, lying on top of a bed of sand, was an ashy charcoal deposit, including the burnt remains of animals but apparently without any human bones. Nonetheless, these bones – which presumably represented animals sacrificed as part of the funeral ceremony – were accompanied by the kinds of finds we'd expect to see in a 'typical' Viking burial: weapons, horse equipment, tools and, of course, a comb. Interestingly, the weapons – a sword, shield and spears – had been deliberately damaged, perhaps to make them useless (either in the afterlife, or to any potential grave robbers), while some of the weapons and horse fittings also showed signs of burning. Had there been some sort of complex cremation cemetery, in which horses and weapons were burnt on the pyre alongside the human body that is now missing? Perhaps the cremated human remains were collected up and taken elsewhere. Whatever the nature of the ritual, one thing is striking: the comb and its case appear to have escaped burning or deliberate destruction, having probably been placed in the mound after the cremation itself was complete. It was clearly important to inter the comb but, for whatever reason, burning it was not seen as appropriate, necessary or desirable. Perhaps, as has been claimed for early Anglo-Saxon cremation, the comb played an important symbolic and mnemonic role in the 'transformation' of the deceased. It is impossible to know for certain. But it meant *something*.

Summary: In Search of Meaning

The myriad ways in which combs were treated in mortuary ritual, together with the fragmentary nature of our evidence, make it impossible to propose any sort of generalising, all-embracing explanation of the phenomenon. However, notwithstanding these problems, it may be possible to make a few general statements about the use of combs in burial practice. The situation in Scandinavia is so varied that it has been necessary to focus on the British Isles herein, and examples from England are too scarce to allow any sort of meaningful generalisation, but we may be able to say a little about the situation in Scotland, where over 130 'Viking' burials are known. Many of these contain combs, and the high level of workmanship they exhibit is testament to the time taken in their manufacture, as well as their perceived value. As we have seen, some such combs may have been created by special commission, or passed on from one magnate to another by means of gift exchange. They may have stood for pacts or alliances between leaders or groups, or they may have formalised clientship or tenancy agreements, familial or marital bonds. Perhaps this is why they ended up in the grave; it signifies something about the end (or the continuation) of a relationship between the deceased and another, unknown, party.

As we have seen for combs in general, the details of how these combs were used are unclear. However, the combs from Scotland's Viking-Age graves do show one common pattern: a lack of evidence of toothwear or breakage, or of any indications of having been repaired. This is in stark contrast to the pattern seen in combs from settlements, whether they be the Brough of Birsay, York or Birka. It might suggest that 'grave combs' were curated for their own sake, and rarely used. Such behaviour is consistent with a role for such combs in formalising alliances, bonds and relationships, though there are other alternatives. It is possible that the combs *were* used, but not on a regular basis. Their 'special' status may have necessitated a similarly specialised use; perhaps in ritualised grooming. As we have seen, saga evidence does suggest that the act of mutual hair combing had a particular intimate component (see Chapters 1 and 4). A further alternative is that the combs were manufactured purely for the purpose of interment. If this was the case, combs could have been curated for many years prior to an individual's death (a possibility which has important implications for their use in dating), or they could have been quickly manufactured soon after the death of the person concerned. This option is perhaps the least likely, for a number of reasons. First, the scale and level of craftsmanship of many of these combs does not sit well with the idea of them being hurried commissions. Second, and more importantly, the simplest explanation for the number of high-quality,

early Viking combs in burials dated to between AD 850 and 950 is that
they represent the personal belongings of the first generations of the early
waves of settlers.

Whatever their role in the world of the living, these combs clearly found
a particular place and function in the land of the dead (or, to put it more
precisely, in mediating the transition between life and death). In an effort
to understand precisely what this role might be, we can do worse than
consider a similar, frequently observed phenomenon in the pagan graves of
early Anglo-Saxon England. In this context, scholars have made interesting
suggestions about the centrality of combs to the rite of cremation burial.[24]
Burial and cremation, of course, are fundamentally about the 'remaking'
of a person's identity. The functional role of items such as combs in the
day-to-day reordering of a person's appearance makes them appropriate
as a symbol for this post-mortem reinvention, thus explaining their
placement *unburnt* in the cremation urn. It is difficult to posit such a role
for combs in Viking-Age burials, as they receive no such special treatment,
and appear to be just one component of a repertoire of appropriate grave
goods. Nonetheless, one may still take something from this theory, and see
furnished burials not as a reflection of the deceased individual's identity,
not as a manifestation of the society in which he lived, nor even simply a
performance put on by those involved in the funeral, but as a 'remaking' of
the dead. The new identity may be informed by the individual's life, and by
the wishes and ideas of his/her kin and peer group, but it is not necessarily
a direct expression of any of these. Thus, the (probably) male child buried
at Balnakeil was 'remade' as an adult warrior or chieftain, complete with
outsized weaponry. His ornate comb may not have ever belonged to him,
but the references it made to Scandinavian identity, status and bonds
of fealty projected the image that someone intended for him: that of a
powerful warrior and a man of power, authority and heritage.

Thus, we have seen that combs were central to complex society, to
negotiating life in the world of the living and to mediating movements
into the world of the dead. Moreover, these roles were fundamentally
linked; the comb's associations with status and identity, with kinship and
fealty, with marking bonds and biography, with transformation and the
maintenance of social boundaries were equally potent in life and in death.
Just as combs started out as part of the architecture of status, and later
found a role as a bridge between the elite and the increasingly mobile
urban populace, so they became established as an important component of
the equipment that eased the transition from this world into the next. Such
is the power and diversity of an object that may seem, on the face of it,
to be straightforward, functional, and one-dimensional. On the contrary,
combs might even be said to move in the fourth dimension, and we might

now investigate the lives of combs beyond their disposal on the ground, in the rubbish or in the grave.

Indeed, for many combs, deposition is not really the end. A number go on to be recovered by archaeologists, researchers and excited students, whereupon they are recorded, photographed, described, discussed, published, curated and displayed. And so begins a new phase in the life of the comb. It would be possible to detail this most recent phase of biography now, but I hope you will see that we have been indirectly tracing the threads of this story since the outset of the book. We have been discussing not just the manufacture, trade, use and deposition of Viking-Age combs, but also the methods by which they are recovered, analysed, interpreted and discussed in the present. Biographies are never linear, and we have now closed the loop on this particular story. The Viking-Age comb still holds a fascination today, not merely for its technological sophistication or aesthetic appeal, but for what it can tell us about the people who made and traded combs, and those who lived and died with them. For many people in Viking-Age society, combs really were a way of life.

FOR KIRKWALL

POOL, SANDAY
COMBS

SCAR, SANDAY, G
(AOC 191)

MAMMAL AND FIS

31. Combs: processed and packaged for research, curation and display. (Image by Steve Ashby, courtesy Orkney Museum).

Notes

1 Introduction

1. See Price 2002.
2. See for instance, Dan Miller's work on contemporary material culture; e.g. Miller 2002, 2005, 2008.
3. See Schama 2010: 394–5.
4. See, for example Edmonds 1999: 8–9.
5. Ambrosiani 1981: 15.
6. Ashby in prep.
7. There is a wide literature on the significance of deer and antler in the past, looked at from a variety of perspectives. See for instance Buckland 1980; Meaney 1981; Hultkrantz 1985; Bath 1992; Green 1992; Hicks 1993.
8. See Galloway and Newcomer 1981 for an accessible overview of the manufacturing method for composite combs, and some experimental work in support of the process.
9. See Williams 2003 for a detailed discussion of combs in Anglo-Saxon burial. See also Chapter 6, this volume.
10. See for instance Owen and Dalland 1999a; Welander *et al.* 1987. See also Chapter 6, this volume.
11. This is a well-established phenomenon; see MacGregor *et al.* 1999: 1938, for example.
12. Documentary evidence also suggests that combs were exchanged in aristocratic circles around this time (see Sherley-Price 1990: 125; Sorrell 1996), and though this does not provide evidence that the practice was widespread, it does give us a way into the subject beyond the purely speculative.

13. Combs are frequently carved on Pictish 'symbol stones'. Much has been written about them, though their meaning in this context is not well understood (see Foster 1990: 162–5).

14. A medieval comb from the Swedish town of Sigtuna bears a well-drawn incised graffito in the form of an image of Christ (Tesch 1987: fig. 8; Smirnova 2005: 244).

15. It has been suggested that certain medieval combs were designed to look like fish, and thus signified the identity of the wealthy fish merchants and 'pirate fishermen' that used them (Clarke and Heald 2002).

16. There is much evidence of this in literature and art. See for instance Jones and Jones 1949: 116–9, 134–5; Ashby in prep.

17. Such rules are known to exist in a wide range of cultures and societies across the globe, and across time (see for example Hall 1654; Frazer 1913; Berg 1951; Leach 1958; Smyser 1965; Douglas 1966; Hallpike 1969, 1979; Derrett 1973; Hershman 1974; Obeyesekere 1981; Ribeiro 1986; Bartlett 1994; Hiltebeitel 1998; Miller 1998; Pohl 1998; Singh 1998; Winstead 2003).

18. The 'biography of objects' approach is well established in archaeological theory, though is still rather inconsistently applied. Good discussions and examples can be found in Appadurai 1986; Kopytoff 1986; Hoskins 1998; Gosden and Marshall 1999; Gilchrist 2012; Joy 2010).

2 Beginnings

1. Olaus Magnus 1555: 18:4.

2. This point, which when baldly stated sounds rather obvious, has been overlooked by archaeologists for years. The idea has recently been eloquently stated in reference to the material culture and art of early prehistoric people (Conneller 2011).

3. There is a wide literature on the biology and zoology of antlers, their growth and their function; the subject continues to perplex scientists today (see Asleson *et al.* 1996; Asleson *et al.* 1997; Azorit *et al.* 2002; Bubenik 1990; Bubenik and Bubenik 1990; Chapman 1975; Chapman 1981; Goss 1969; Goss 1995; Huxley 1926; Huxley 1931; Kierdorf *et al.* 2000; Kierdorf *et al.* 1995; Li *et al.* 2003; Lincoln and Fletcher 1984; Lincoln 1992; MacEwen 1920; Muir and Sykes 1988; Schmidt *et al.* 2001).

4. This has important implications for the manufacture of antler objects, as ground-breaking physical tests (undertaken by archaeologists and biologists in tandem) have shown (MacGregor and Currey 1983).

5. See MacGregor and Currey 1983.
6. This idea is another raised by Conneller (2011) in her work on the early Stone Age.
7. This issue has caused some problems in the study of animal biogeography, when historical accounts are drawn upon. For a time, accounts of Scottish reindeer in *Orkneyinga Saga* caused some debate in academic circles (see Anderson 1999: 182).
8. The early geography of red deer is well covered by Sommer *et al.* 2008.
9. The behaviour of deer populations is discussed by Mitchell *et al.* 1977: 3.
10. See Mitchell *et al.* 1977: 3, 41; see also Chapman 1975.
11. On the history of deer hunting, see Almond 2003; Cummins 1988; Sykes 2005, 2007, 2010.
12. Pliny's evocative discussion of deer behaviour is recounted by Rackham 1940: 73, 81–87; see also Hassig 1995: 40–51.
13. Though it has never really been picked up or elaborated upon, the importance of such knowledge has been noted previously. See for instance Christophersen's (1980: 157) account of medieval combmaking in Lund.
14. This trend is apparent in the worked bone reports from many of the key early medieval urban sites of Europe (see Ambrosiani 1981: 52, 98; MacGregor *et al.* 1999: 1906–9; Mann 1982: 37–38; Reichstein 1969: 62; but compare Smirnova 1997: 139).
15. Such physical and biological insults are well evidenced in archaeological material, but have also been observed at first hand in the wild (see MacGregor 1985: 36; Sutcliffe 1973a; 1973b; 1974; *cf.* Brothwell 1976).
16. See Olaus Magnus 1555: 18:4.
17. The importance of learned experience to surviving in a given society is a subject well studied by British social anthropologists such as Tim Ingold (e.g. Ingold 1993, 2000).
18. Such discussions are rarely found in the academic literature, but may be chanced upon on the internet, and in hobby magazines and specialist books (see, for example, Mason 2008).
19. These ideas, identified by hunters and stalkers themselves, have been discussed in a broader perspective by anthropologists and philosophers for some time. The classic work is by Polanyi (1967).
20. See Mason 2008: 38.
21. This again has resonance with the theoretical literature; see Conneller's (2011: 58–70) work on the nature of the human–animal relationship in early prehistory.

22. This idea was proposed by Kristina Ambrosiani (1981: 40), but see also MacGregor 1985: 36, and compare Cnotliwy 1956: 312.

23. The zooarchaeologist Naomi Sykes has undertaken much recent research into the medieval aristocratic engagement with deer (Sykes 2010), and with attempt to control access to them as a hunting resource (Sykes 2005, 2007).

24. Contrary to popular perception, the concept of the forest pre-dates the Norman Conquest, though the legal and logistical implications of this are unclear. A lack of documentary evidence means that we are very largely reliant on archaeological evidence, though post-Conquest documents such as Domesday Book do allow us to tentatively steal a glimpse of the late Viking-Age arrangement. I should express my thanks to Rob Liddiard for discussion on this point.

25. See Sykes 2010 for an interesting theoretical take on the social context for this 'closing off' of access.

26. See above, and again see Mason 2008.

27. See Kitchener 2010: 40 for habitat, diet and behaviour of elk.

28. See Kitchener 2010: 38 for more on the behaviour of elk under predation.

29. See Stickney 2011 for a 'beginner's guide' to finding shed elk antler.

30. Historic accounts of hunting are useful in characterising wildlife trends; see for instance Salvesen 1929.

31. See Jordhøy 2008 for an account of the evidence for Viking-Age and medieval pit traps in the region.

32. This idea was raised by Kristina Ambrosiani in her seminal work on combmaking in Birka and Ribe (Ambrosiani 1981: 52).

33. Scholars such as Kitchener (2010: 39) have invoked this property of elk antler in explaining its relatively low representation in the early archaeological record.

34. This point was made strongly by Ambrosiani (1981: 34), but is refuted by Callmer (1998: 475), who does not believe raw material to have been the only controlling factor involved in governing comb form.

35. See Heikura *et al.* 1985; Rankama and Ukkonen 2001 and references therein for detailed discussion of the species' ancient distribution.

36. See Paine 1988: 32 for information on reindeer diet.

37. See Ingold 1980: 21 and Paine 1988: 34 for discussion on reindeer herd behaviour, and the role of the antlers of the female.

38. See Paine 1988: 34 for discussion on reindeer migration, thermoregulation and the pest of insects.

39. See Paine 1988: 34 on migration and herd size.

40. See Ingold 1980: 22 on tundra and woodland reindeer.

41. Paine 1988: 32.
42. See Ingold 1980: 46 on the mutability of migration routes.
43. See Ingold 1980: 53 on the difficulty of finding reindeer in the wild.
44. See Ingold 1980: 49 on the difficulty of 'following' reindeer.
45. See Burch 1972: 345.
46. See Ingold 1980: 54–5 on the logistics of such a strategy.
47. See Ingold 1980: 53.
48. See Bergman *et al.* 2007: 399 for a discussion of the dangers of early medieval Arctic and subarctic navigation.
49. Bergman *et al.* 2007 recounts the details of this unusual archaeological discovery.
50. This is a highly charged debate, in political, ethnic and archaeological terms. See Odner 1985; Odner 1992; Olsen 1985; Olsen 2003; Price 2002; Storli 1993; Zachrisson 2008 for a flavour of the seriousness and contemporary importance of the argument.
51. See Ingold 1980: 22 on harvesting deer hide, and seasonality.
52. Indrelid and Hufthammer 2011 recount the archaeological and historical evidence for this activity.
53. See Barth 1983; Blehr 1973; Indrelid and Hufthammer 2011; Jordhøy 2008 for accounts of this landscape of trapping.
54. See Jordhøy 2008 on pit alignment.
55. See Ingold 1980: 57 on the relationship between technology and environment.
56. See Ingold 1980: 64–5 on the use of 'decoy' reindeer in hunting strategies.
57. See Paine 1988: 33 on reindeer migration and topography.
58. See Burch 1972 for a full discussion.
59. See Ingold 1980: 75 on biting insects.
60. See Paine 1988: 33 on food availability, snow cover and reindeer behaviour.
61. See Bergman *et al.* 2007: 397–8 on the origins of the Saami.
62. See Aronsson 1991; Storli 1993 on the antiquity of Saami reindeer hunting.
63. See Äikäs *et al.* 2009 on Saami cosmology.
64. Ingold 1980: 281–2; see also Paine 1971: 164.
65. Ingold 1980: 282.
66. See Bradley 2000: 1–14; Äikäs *et al.* 2009; Salmi *et al.* 2011 for discussions of *Sjedde* shrines.
67. The idea of a constructed 'Other' with which a society opposes itself comes, of course, from Edward Said's *Orientalism* (1978).
68. See Hultkrantz 1985; Ingold 2000: 89–152; Price 2002 on the Saami and Shamanic cosmologies.

69. See Ingold 1980: 264–86 on social differentiation in Saami populations.
70. The operation of such an architecture of power is well attested in medieval Europe. For recent accounts, see for instance Steane 2001; Sykes 2010.
71. See Ingold 1980: 267.
72. See Olsen 2003 for a full discussion of the likely nature of early medieval Norse–Saami interaction.
73. See Ingold 1980: 268 on *stallo* sites.
74. See Aronsson 1993; Carpelan 1993; Storli 1993 for *stallo* sites in a (partially) pastoral context.
75. See Carpelan 1993 for *stallo* sites and Norse–Saami interaction.
76. See Cameron 1998.
77. See Ingold 1980: 73 on the economics of deer meat, skin and winter subsistence.
78. See Christensen 1987 for the 'hunter-combmakers'.
79. Excavations at this key site have recently been published; see Weber 2007.
80. Mature bulls shed first; see Paine 1988: 34.
81. For discussions of antlerworking and combmaking at this important town, see Rytter 2001; Vretemark 1989; Vretemark 1997.
82. This story is recounted in the *Saga of Olaf the Holy* (Hollander 1995: 432).
83. See Blehr 1973; Hambleton and Rowley-Conwy 1997 for the hunting landscapes of early medieval Norway.
84. There is little consensus on the timing of the transition from hunting to herding, even in very broad terms. Compare the views of Odner 1993; Storli 1993, 1996; and Walleström 2000 on this matter.
85. See Ingold 1980; Jackson and Thacker 1997; Took 2004 for accounts of the 'herding' way of life.
86. Most notably Storli 1993.
87. See Aronsson 1993; Carpelan 1993; Hansen 1993; Mulk 1993; Odner 1993. Storli points out that we have yet to establish a clear relationship between the *stallo* sites and their ostensibly associated trapping systems, but neither is clear evidence of a pastoral relationship forthcoming, and Knut Odner (1993) has pointed out the possibility that many forms of hunting would be archaeologically invisible. Storli also argues that the lack of evidence for the significance of reindeer skins in the Viking-Age fur trade renders untenable the interpretation of *stallo* sites as settlements related to large-scale trapping. However, neither do the documentary sources offer any real support for early pastoralism, and, as we have seen,

reindeer antler must have been an important tradeable material; if not recorded in documentary sources, the clearest indication of this is the growing trade in antler combs.

88. See Carpelan 1993 for arguments around this point.
89. See Ingold 1980: 77 for the explanation behind this argument.
90. See Storli 1993: 14.
91. See Ingold 1980: 78, 268 on culling strategies.
92. It should be noted, however, that the detailed impact of the process is poorly understood (see Lincoln and Fletcher 1984; Lincoln 1992; Kierdorf *et al.* 1995 for example).
93. See, for example Flodin 1989; Vretemark 1997.
94. This idea is not completely new; Christophersen (1980), as we have seen, has suggested that the provisioning of combmaking in medieval Lund must have been dependent on a good understanding of reindeer, their behaviour, and their habitat, though the implications have never really been thought through in detail.
95. See contemporary accounts of shed collecting (e.g. Mason 2008: 38).
96. See Edmonds 2004: 153–70 for discussions around this concept.

3 Ways of Working, Ways of Making

1. Meyer 1906: 13.
2. We might even suggest that technology actually made humans; that the development of tools allowed us to behave, and ultimately evolve in new ways; see Taylor 2010.
3. See, for example Bradley and Edmonds 2005; Edmonds 1995; Kohn and Mithen 1999.
4. It has been argued that grooming – as a social behaviour – played a fundamental role in the development of language; see Dunbar 1998. Some chimpanzees even clean themselves using leaves as sponges; see Whiten *et al.* 1999.
5. Conneller 2011
6. Conneller 2004.
7. See for example Ashby and Bolton 2010.
8. It is clear that toothcutting invariably took place after assembly, as toothcuts are frequently observed on the basal edges of connecting plates. Interestingly, experiment has shown that with care and experience comb teeth can be cut relatively safely and efficiently, so that the risk of breakage is manageable; see Galloway and Newcomer 1981: 80–82.
9. See Lemonnier 1993a: 2, 16.

10. See for example Bijker and Law 1994; Pinch and Bijker 1987; see also historical and archaeological work such as Dobres 2000; Geselowitz 1993; Hughes 1994; Sinclair and Schlanger 1990.
11. See Conneller 2011.
12. See Van der Leeuw 1993.
13. Compare MacGregor 1985; Zurowski 1974.
14. See Galloway and Newcomer 1981.
15. *cf.* Edmonds 1999: 15–31 for a similar way of conceptualising the production of stone tools.
16. See Ashby 2006: 99–128; Ashby in prep-a; *cf.* Ambrosiani 1981; Flodin 1989
17. Ashby in press-a.
18. See Pinch and Bijker 1987.
19. See Cnoliwy 1973; Ulbricht 1978, 1980; Ambrosiani 1981; Christophersen 1980; MacGregor *et al.* 1999; Hansen 2005; Smirnova 2005; Ashby 2006.
20. See Ulbricht 1978.
21. See Ambrosiani 1981; Nicholson 1997; Callmer 2002; Hansen 2005.
22. See Sindbaek 2007a, 2007b, 2008.
23. See Callmer 2002.
24. See Drew 1965.
25. Hudson-Edwards *et al.* 1999a, 1999b.
26. On itinerancy, see Ashby 2006, 2012.
27. See Ambrosiani 1981.
28. See Ulriksen 1998, 2004.
29. See Carver 1990.
30. See Abrams 2012 for a discussion of this way of thinking about the Viking-Age migrations.
31. See Callmer 2003 for a thoughtful discussion of the life and perceptions of the smith in early medieval Scandinavia.
32. See Dunlevy 1988 for a reference in the eighth-century *Vision of Adamnan* to there being a space in hell reserved for dishonest combmakers, and Drew 1965 on the drunken combmakers of nineteenth-century Kenilworth!
33. See Callmer 2002 for arguments around this theme.

4 Technologies of Transformation

1. Smyser 1965.
2. *Alcuin's Letter to Ethelred*, Wattenbach and Diimler 1873: 131.

3. See Wylie 1985.
4. Frazer 1913.
5. Berg 1951: 82–94.
6. Leach 1958.
7. Hallpike 1969.
8. 1 Corinthians: 11:3–16.
9. Derrett 1973.
10. Leach 1958: 150.
11. Archer 1946: 316, also 219, 252; Singh 1998.
12. Leach 1958: 151, 158.
13. See for example the biblical story of Samson (Judges 16:17); *cf.* Goosmann 2012.
14. See Singh 1998; Bartlett 1994; see also Miller 1998: 284.
15. Obeyesekere 1981: 50–51.
16. Aldhouse-Green 2004a and 2004b; compare the famous naturalist Dian Fossey's attitude to hair and its magical misuse in Rwanda (Gourevitch 1999: 77–8).
17. In those cases in which human hair is preserved as a fibre, it has frequently been a subject of both analytical and theoretical focus; see for example the work undertaken on hair from bodies preserved in peat bogs (Wilson, Richards *et al.* 2007; see also Aldhouse-Green 2004b: 302) or by mummification (Fletcher 2005; Wilson *et al.* 2007).
18. See Gansum 1993; Fletcher 2005: 20; Bickle 2007; Cleland *et al.* 2005; Eckardt and Crummy 2008; Hamilakis *et al.* 2002; Joyce 2005; Reischer and Koo 2004; Schildkrout 2004; Sofaer 2006.
19. Aldhouse-Green 2004b.
20. Bartman 2001.
21. Wilson, Richards *et al.* 2007; Wilson, Taylor *et al.* 2007.
22. Ingold 2000; Merleau-Ponty 1962; Gibson 1979.
23. Shove 2003; Heilscher 2011.
24. Olivelle 1998: 11–49; see also Bartlett 1994: 60.
25. Miller 1998.
26. See Frazer 1915; Leach 1958; Hallpike 1969.
27. Douglas 1966; Hershman 1974; Obeyesekere 1981; Olivelle 1998.
28. Wilken, cited in Leach 1958: 149; *cf.* Hallpike 1969.
29. White 2006.
30. Dunbar 1998.
31. See Edmonds 1995 (e.g. pages 77, 152) for the association of stone tools with burials and the body.
32. Fletcher 2005.
33. Fletcher 2000.

34. Robins 1999.
35. Joy 2010.
36. Derks and Vos 2010: 68.
37. Derks and Vos 2010: 65.
38. Dutton 2004: 4.
39. Dutton 2004: 5.
40. Dutton 2004: 9. This passage synthesises a rather fuller and more in-depth discussion in Dutton's *Charlemagne's Mustache*. Please refer to this for a fuller account.
41. Dutton 2004: 9.
42. Dutton 2004: 10.
43. See Foster 1990, for instance.
44. Williams 2003, 2004, 2007.
45. James 1988: 142.
46. Dutton 2004: 12; Fischer Drew 1949: 26, 45, 82.
47. Dutton 2004: 11–12.
48. Dutton 2004: 4.
49. Dutton 2004: 13–14.
50. See also Fischer Drew 1949.
51. *cf.* Wallace-Hadrill 1982; Goosmann 2012.
52. Dutton 2004: 23.
53. See Gansum 1993.
54. This material is held by the Statens Historiska Museet, Stockholm, Sweden (SHM 16171); Rydh 1936.
55. Sheppard 1904: 51; see also Gansum 1993.
56. Barrett 2008.
57. A detailed survey of references to hair in medieval documents was recently published by Bartlett (1994).
58. Callow 2006; see *Orkneyinga Saga*, Chapters 66 and 71 (Anderson 1999: 102–3, 113).
59. Tschan 2002. See also Anglo-Saxon literature, such as Asser's *Life of King Alfred* (Keynes and Lapidge 1983); *cf. The Song of Roland* (Terry 1965).
60. Pohl 1998.
61. Note also that a similar formula can be found in the Anglo-Saxon Chronicle (for example references to the 'fair hair'd youth' and 'fair hair'd hero', entries for AD 938 and AD 975; see Ingram 1912: 86, 97 or Baker, 2000: 79, 84) in *The Song of Roland* (see Terry 1965: 6), and in Saxo Grammaticus' *History of the Danes* (Fisher 1979: 208).
62. *The Story of Harald Hairfair* (*Harald Harfager's Saga*), Chapter 23 (Morris and Magnússon 1893, 117).

63. Reported by Tacitus; see Aldhouse-Green 2004b for a discussion.
64. Sigurðson 2007.
65. The *Poetic* and *Prose Edda* are thirteenth-century Icelandic texts relating Norse mythology, origin stories, and other tales, but which contain elements of earlier oral traditions, arguably preserved since the Viking Age. It is also notable that hair plays an important part in this Norse creation myth; the first part of a man to be created is his hair, even before his head (See Faulkes 2002: 96–7 for the mythological derivation of this literary device), and that in Eddic poetry, gold may be referred to as 'Sif's hair'.
66. *Heimskringla, the Saga of Harald Hardrada*, Chapter 19 (see Laing and Rhys 1930, 19).
67. Bede, *Ecclesiastical History of the English People*, Sherley-Price 1990: 103.
68. *Heimskringla, Magnus Barefoot's Saga*, Chapters 18, 53. Laing and Rhys 1930: 269–70.
69. *Njal's Saga*, Chapter 44. Magnusson and Pálsson 1960: 114.
70. *Njal's Saga*, Chapter 77. Magnusson and Pálsson 1960: 171.
71. *The Tale of Audun from the West Fjords*, Chapter 2 (Smiley 2000: 719); cf. *The Saga of the People of Laxardal*, Chapter 64 (Smiley 2000: 393).
72. Fisher 1979: 270.
73. *Hakon the Good's Saga*, 31. *The Fall of Eyvind Braggart and Alf Ashman*, 59. Morris and Magnússon 1893: 186; see also *Heimskringla, The Story of Olaf the Holy, the Son of Harald*, Chapter 193, 60. Morris and Magnússon 1894: 373.
74. *Heimskringla, The Story of Olaf the Holy, the Son of Harald* Chapter 14, 60. Morris and Magnússon 1894: 17.
75. *Heimskringla, The Story of Olaf the Holy, the Son of Harald* Chapter 47, 60 (Morris and Magnússon 1894: 58).
76. *Heimskringla, The Story of King Olaf Tryggvison* Chapter 46, 59 (Morris and Magnússon 1894: 281).
77. See *The Story of Olaf the Holy, the Son of Harald*, Chapter 259 (Morris and Magnússon 1894: 457–60).
78. Faulkes 2002: 53.
79. Fisher 1979: 189, 195, 226.
80. See in particular the frequent references to Charlemagne's moustache and beard in the *Song of Roland* [lines 248–50, 970, 4001] (Terry 1965: 13, 40, 146). See also Dutton 2004.
81. See the *Edda* (Faulkes 2002); *Orkneyinga Saga*, Chapters 46, 47, 75, 80 (Anderson 1999: 71–2; 119–20; 135) *Saxo Grammaticus* (Fisher 1979: 280); *The Saga of the People of Vatnsdal*, Chapters

45, 58 (Smiley 2000: 329, 404, 418); *Gisli Sursson's Saga* (Smiley 2000: 515, 517, 552); *The Saga of the Greenlanders*, Chapters 6, 58. (Smiley 2000: 647); *Eirik the Red's Saga*, Chapter 4 (Smiley 2000: 658); *The Tale of Sarcastic Halli*, Chapter 2 (Smiley 2000: 695).

82. Smiley 2000: 357–66.
83. Sindbaek 2011.
84. Bede, *Ecclesiastical History of the English People* (Sherley-Price 1990: 264–5); *cf. The Song of Roland* (Terry 1965: 88).
85. See Fry 1981.
86. See for example Aelfric's *Letter to the Monks of Eynsham* (Jones 1998).
87. Vaughan 1958: 60.
88. See also *Saxo Grammaticus* (Fisher 1979: 155).
89. See Sherley-Price 1990: 187, 189, 203; Ceolfrid's letter to the Picts (Sherley-Price 1990: 317–21).
90. Heilscher 2011: 53.
91. Heilscher 2011; see also Shove 2003.
92. Heilscher 2011: 223.
93. Heilscher 2011: 125–7.
94. Heilscher 2011: 163.
95. Gell 1992.
96. Zahavi and Zahavi 1997.
97. Ashby 2002.
98. Douglas 1966.

5 Combs and Communities

1. Sorrell 1996.
2. Olivelle 1998.
3. Shawcross 1964.
4. See for example Mumcuoglu and Zias 1989; Schelvis 1994.
5. My thanks to Harry Kenward for discussion on this point.
6. MacGregor 1985: 78.
7. Lasko 1956.
8. Brett 1956; Flanagan 1956; Kitzinger 1956.
9. Whitelock 1979: 473.
10. See Higgitt 1995.
11. Sherley-Price 1990.
12. See Sorrell 1996.
13. See for example Higgitt 1987.
14. Hall and Whyman 1996: 125, 127–8.

15. See above; James 1988: 142–4.
16. Foster 1990.
17. See Cummins 1999.
18. Joy 2010.
19. McIntyre 1929.
20. Soulat 2011.
21. See Graham-Campbell 1985.
22. Riddler 1998; see Riddler 1990 for a wider survey of the 'handled' type.
23. Terry 1965.
24. See Meaney 1981 on the 'magical' and cosmological associations of antler objects.
25. Hollander 1949.
26. MacGregor 1985: 82.
27. See, for example Sigurðson 2007.
28. See Paterson 2012 (and references therein). Paterson presents an excellent interdisciplinary study of the complex relationships between dress, identity and power in early medieval Britain.
29. Ashby in press-a.
30. Clarke and Heald 2002.
31. Sharples 2003.
32. See Flodin 1989; Haigh 1871: 278–81; Okasha 1999.
33. Ashby in press-b.
34. *Skaldsparmal*, Faulkes (trans.) 2002: 103.
35. *Erbyggja* Saga, Chapter 28. Pálsson and Edwards 1972: 78–9.
36. See Radford 1959.
37. DuBois 1999: 100–101.
38. Compare, for example, Paterson 2012.
39. Smith 2003.
40. See Vretemark 1997.

6 Ends

1. Smiley 2000: 279.
2. Wallace 1693.
3. Gibson and Bradford 2008.
4. See Owen and Dalland 1999.
5. Further details of this, and other Scottish burials discussed in this chapter, are accessibly summarised in Graham-Campbell and Batey 1998.
6. See Price 2010.

7. These ideas are discussed at length (in an early Anglo-Saxon context) by Howard Williams; see Williams 2003, 2004, 2006, 2007.

8. See MacGregor 1985: 77–8, fig. 44d-g.

9. Williams 2004.

10. Chapter 55; see Smiley 2000: 381.

11. See Wilson 1992: 139–40.

12. See Williams 2003.

13. See for example Ambrosiani 1981; Alexander 1987; Owen and Dalland 1999; Eldjárn 2000.

14. Note the historically documented scissors associated with the comb in the grave of St Cuthbert; see Battiscombe 1956, though the date at which they may have been interred is subject to debate (see Lasko 1956: 340).

15. Holmquist Olausson 1990.

16. We await the final report; see Graham-Campbell and Batey 1998: 140–42 for an effective summary.

17. See Graham-Campbell and Batey 1998: 135–8; see also Kaland 1993.

18. Thorsteinsson 1968.

19. Ambrosiani 1981: 24.

20. Svanberg 2003.

21. Lyasight 1971.

22. Alexander 1987.

23. Hodgson 1832.

24. Williams 2003.

Glossary

Below are explanations of some of the key terms used in the text, together with places, concepts and names of the key players. Particularly for the more theoretical terms, these are certainly not definitive, but rather represent personal interpretations, signifying the ways in which the terms are used in this book.

Antler. The bony outgrowths found on the heads of deer. Structurally, antler is a complex material, but consists of a tough outer layer of **compacta**, around a core of **spongy, porous tissue**. It is grown rapidly, and shed each year. The antlers of the red deer, reindeer and elk constitute the key raw materials in the manufacture of Viking-Age composite combs, and may be acquired through hunting (butchered antler), or collected from the ground (shed or cast antler).

Anthropology. The study of humans. Of particular interest herein are social and cultural approaches to anthropology, which are concerned with individual and group behaviour and social structure. **Ethnographic** studies of present-day non-Western societies can often yield useful if indirect insights about life in the past.

Alcuin. A senior eighth-century religious scholar and commentator from **York** who became an important figure at the court of **Charlemagne** in Aachen (now Germany). His writings provide one of the key sources of evidence for the Viking raids of Anglo-Saxon monasteries, though it must be remembered that they were written with a particular political and religious agenda, as well as from Charlemagne's court, so do not represent direct personal experience.

Billets. These are the small plates of antler upon which teeth are cut. A number of billets are arranged alongside one another, sandwiched between a pair of connecting plates. Teeth are then cut on the billets, forming **toothplates** and **endplates** (see **composite comb**).

Birka. One of the most important trading centres of Viking-Age Scandinavia, serving travel and exchange across the Baltic and beyond to Russia, Byzantium and the Near East. Birka seems to have been a strikingly cosmopolitan settlement on the island of Björkö, Lake Mälaren, not far from modern-day Stockholm. Archaeological excavations have uncovered an uncommonly rich range of finds from the settlement area (the 'Black Earth') and surrounding gravefields. Following Ingrid Ulbricht's study of the bone and antler waste from Haithabu, Kristina Ambrosiani's work at **Birka** and **Ribe** was of key significance in the development of comb studies; Ambrosiani challenged Ulbricht's view that combmakers spent a portion of their time working on other crafts, and suggested instead that they were full-time but *itinerant* professionals. This view still prevails in much of early medieval archaeology.

Brough of Birsay. A tidal island off the coast of the west mainland of **Orkney**. It is home to Pictish and Norse settlements and, from the Viking Age at least, appears to have been something of a power centre.

Bede. One of the most important scholars and writers of his age (the late seventh and early eighth centuries), 'the Venerable Bede' was a monk based at the monastery of Monkwearmouth and Jarrow in Northumbria, and is best known today for his *Historia ecclesiastica gentis Anglorum* (*The Ecclesiastical History of the English People*). In writing a history of English settlement and political development, this document was central to the formation of an English identity. Herein, it provides a key source for understanding the lives and attitudes of the pre-Viking age, albeit through the eyes of a religious scholar.

Burr. The basal end of an **antler**; the point at which it attaches to the pedicle of the skull.

Beam. This is the central trunk of an **antler**. At its base is the **burr**, at its tip the **crown**, while **tines** branch out along its length. In certain species, the beam may splay into wide, palmated areas.

Connecting plate. See **composite comb**.

Composite comb. The most commonly preserved form of comb from Viking-Age archaeological contexts. Composite combs are composed of a number of components, two (or more) **connecting plates**, between which are ranged a number of **toothplates** and **endplates**.

Coppergate (see **York**). A well-excavated and important site for the understanding of Scandinavian England. Coppergate seems to have been the mercantile centre of tenth- and eleventh-century York, as archaeological excavations have uncovered evidence of a number of crafts and trades.

Carolingian. A Frankish dynasty that rose to power in the late seventh century, ultimately deposing the Merovingian kings of Frankia in AD 751. Their period of rule, which lasted until the tenth century, was one of considerable political success, particularly under the Emperor Charlemagne, and the term 'Carolingian' has come to stand as a chronological label, and a descriptor for certain styles of material culture, as well as a political term.

Cuthbert, St. St Cuthbert is the patron saint of the north of England. His life as a seventh-century monk, ecclesiastic and hermit was celebrated throughout the Middle Ages, and his tomb, now in Durham Cathedral, was venerated for centuries.

Cist. A form of grave architecture, consisting of a stone-lined, rectilinear chamber within which the remains of the dead are interred; a sort of stone-built box or coffin.

Compacta. One of the components of **antler**; this is dense, hard material that lies outside the spongy core, but under the roughly textured surface. The compacta was the material of most use to the antlerworker, and was what composite combs were made from.

Display-side convention. Certain forms of comb are decorated only on one face, suggesting that the comb was intended to be viewed only from one direction, and perhaps that it was worn as an item of dress. It has been suggested that this convention is of **Frisian** origin. Examples of such form are known in Viking-Age England and Scandinavia, though they do not dominate there.

Edda. A collection of Nordic mythological and literary material, in prose and poetic form. Written down in the thirteenth century, it is thought to preserve material passed down by oral tradition from many years previously.

Endplates. The small rectangular pieces of antler that make up the endstops for the central range of a **composite comb**. A row of **billets** are sandwiched between a pair of **connecting plates**, they are then riveted together, and teeth are cut onto them, forming **toothplates** and **endplates**. The endplates may not have teeth cut along their whole length, with an area reserved for a handhold at the terminal. Teeth may be graduated in length to form decorative curves, and flat faces and edges may be ornamented with incised or punched motifs.

Ethnography. This is the study of existing human societies, through direct observation and engagement (through interviews etc.). It is often used as the basis for broader social analogy in **anthropology** and archaeology.

Frankia. A kingdom in western continental Europe, best known for its **Merovingian** and **Carolingian** dynasties. Its extent and power grew between the start of the early Middle Ages and the tenth century, by which point it extended to cover parts of Germany and Italy, as well as present-day France.

Frisia. The coastal area of western continental Europe, roughly covering the region between the Netherlands and north-western Germany, as far as the modern Danish border. The region was extremely important in the early medieval period, when it is thought that Frisian merchants and craftspeople played an important part in northern European trade.

Gift exchange/gift economy. Well studied by anthropologists and ethnographers working in contemporary non-western societies, this term refers to an economy in which gifts are given with an explicit understanding that it must be reciprocated. Such an economy is thought to have occurred in many past societies, including that of early medieval northern Europe. Gifts would also have been given as a means of pledging allegiance or alliance, and as a way of ensuring loyalty among one's followers.

Haithabu/Hedeby. A town now in Germany, but previously belonging to Denmark. It lies in Schleswig-Holstein, on the border between Germany and Danish Jutland. In the Viking Age it was an important trading site, being located at the nexus of the North Sea, the western Baltic, Scandinavia and northern continental Europe. Together with Kristina

Ambrosiani's study of combs and combmaking at **Birka** and **Ribe**, Ingrid Ulbricht's 1978 study of the bone and antler waste from Haithabu was seminal in the field. Ulbricht suggested that combmakers worked on multiple crafts; they may be part time combmakers, part-time amber-workers (for instance).

Hardangervidda. This mountain plateau, the largest in Europe, lies in western Norway. It offers an alpine, partially glaciated environment, and is home to a distinctive fauna, including thousand-strong herds of reindeer. It has thus long been an important ground for hunting, and seems to have supplied the combmaking industry of medieval Bergen with considerable quantities of antler.

Itinerancy. Archaeologists frequently suggest that certain crafts were carried out by travelling artisans. This is the received wisdom for the organisation of Viking-Age combmaking, though we should not accept such models uncritically, but be open to the possibility of regional and chronological variation in logistics and practical organisation.

Ibn Fadlan was a tenth-century Kurdish traveller who visited the Volga region as an ambassador for the Abbasid Caliphate in Baghdad. His accounts provide a key resource for our understanding of 'Viking' societies in the east, including burial ritual and grooming behaviour.

Kaupang (strictly 'market') in Skiringssal, southern Norway was a key trading site in early Viking-Age Scandinavia, and is often raised as an example of one of the region's first towns. It dates back to the later eighth century, though survived for just over 100 years. Merchants travelling the Baltic circuit would have been very familiar with Kaupang, and recent excavations are starting to reveal much about craft, trade, and life there.

Laxdaela Saga is a well-known Icelandic saga, telling stories of life in the Breiðafjörður region of Iceland. In common with other sagas, it was written in the thirteenth century, but tells stories situated in the ninth, tenth, and eleventh centuries.

Merovingian. The Merovingian kings ruled Frankia between the fifth century and the mid-eighth, at which point they were usurped by the mayors of their palace, and what was to become the Carolingian dynasty.

Njal's Saga is an Icelandic saga written in the thirteenth century, but referred to events (chiefly bloodfeud) that ostensibly took place between the late tenth and early eleventh century. It is thus a useful, if problematic source for the study of the Viking Age.

Orkney. A group of islands off the north coast of Scotland. Together with the Shetland Islands, it makes up the Northern Isles. Orkney may seem small and distant, but in the Viking Age and Middle Ages it was far from peripheral and insignificant. It is often characterised as an important stopping-off point on the 'Sea Road' from Norway to the islands of the North Atlantic, but it was in fact much more than that; in many ways it was almost an independent kingdom, and as result of trade and piracy it became powerful and wealthy.

Olaus Magnus was a sixteenth-century scholar best known for his *Historia de Gentibus Septentrionalibus (History of the Northern Peoples)*, a patriotic and widely translated work on the folklore, customs and manners of the people of Scandinavia. It can be seen as a useful, if problematic, ethnohistoric source.

Olaf, St. Olaf II Haraldsson was King of Norway between 1015 and 1028. His life and miracles are documented in a range of sources, but his role in the Christianisation of Norway is far from assured, and he was certainly not your traditional, peace-loving saint; his reign is most notable for the expansion of power over the various petty kings of Norway. He was exiled by Cnut of Denmark in 1029, and ultimately killed at the Battle of Stiklestad in 1030. He was subsequently canonised, and made patron saint of Norway. A small number of English churches bear dedications to St Olaf or St Olave, and thus stand as testament to the Scandinavian legacy on the British Isles.

Rivets. Metal studs used to fix together the various elements of a **composite comb**. The rivets could be iron, rolled copper-alloy sheet, or copper-plated iron. Bone and antler pegs are also known, while the placement of rivet also shows considerable variation according to regional manufacturing tradition, sometimes being used for decorative effect.

Ribe. Today, Ribe is a small town in western Jutland, Denmark, but in the early Viking Age it was one of the most important trading settlements in Scandinavia, linking the Baltic with the North Sea. Alongside Kaupang, Birka, Hedeby and Dorestad, it belongs to an 'elite' group of trading towns that anchored mercantile activity in northern Europe.

Rus. A term variously used for the early medieval state founded in the later ninth century and centred on Novgorod, and for the traders and settlers of the region. The ethnic identity and homogeneity of the group has been much debated, but the group no doubt emerged from the coming together of Scandinavians and Slavs.

Saami. The indigenous people of Arctic Eurasia, particularly northern Scandinavia and Russia.

Seidr. A set of magical beliefs and practices associated with the Saami, often thought to contain elements of shamanism and animism.

Spongy Tissue (see **antler**). Also referred to as 'cancellous tissue'. Antler consists of two forms of bone: a dense, hard outer *compacta* (the material from which combs and other artefacts are made), and a much softer, more open (and technologically less useful) core.

Song of Roland (*Chanson de Roland*). An eleventh-century French poem, recounting the heroic story of an eighth-century battle.

Stallo **sites.** This is the name given to small, upland settlements in Scandinavia, consisting of just two to three buildings and hearths within an area encircled by a raised bank. Their function and significance has been much debated, but they are frequently implicated in arguments surrounding the questions of Norse–Saami interaction, and the transition from hunting society to reindeer pastoralism.

Sunken feature buildings (**SFBs, see also Grubenhäuser**) are frequently encountered structures on early medieval settlements. They are small structures, cut into the earth, with timber posts to support their roofs. They may have had functions as dwellings, workshops or storage buildings.

Technology. Herein a rather broad definition is taken, to include not just processes of craft and manufacture, but any form of skilled practice, even those that are apparently 'second nature' (see Ingold 2000).

Theoderic the Great. Fifth- and sixth-century King of the Ostrogoths, the powerful 'barbarian' society that held hegemony over south-eastern Europe in the middle of the first millennium AD. His successes included establishing rule over Italy. He was held up as a barbarian hero for centuries after his death.

Tines. Colloquially referred to as 'points', tines branch off from the main **beam** of an **antler**. Moving upwards from the **burr**, they may be referred to as the first, second and third or brow, bez and trez tines.

Toothplates. The small rectangular pieces of antler that make up the central range of a **composite comb**. A row of **billets** are sandwiched between a pair of **connecting plates**, they are then riveted together, and teeth are cut onto them, forming **toothplates** and **endplates**.

Viking. The word 'Viking' is so vaguely defined that it is difficult to use in any meaningful way. Do we mean raiders? Or just Scandinavians? Do we include the 'Anglo-Scandinavian' or 'Hiberno-Norse' offspring of Scandinavian settlers? For these reasons, herein the term is not used to directly refer to people.

Viking Age. Demarking the limits of the Viking Age is not straightforward, as it varies not just with geography but also according to the criteria used to define it. Simple equations such as the period of Scandinavian overlordship or influence do not work well; northern Scotland, for instance, was under Scandinavian rulership long after its experience could be considered in any way 'Viking'. Instead, one may focus (for instance) on political conquest, piratical activity, on Scandinavian state formation, economic or political expansion, religious reform and conversion, the development of trade and urbanism or the use of particular forms of material culture. Each of these phenomena would allow the dates of the Viking Age to be defined in different ways. For the sake of convenience, in the British Isles the start of the Viking Age is often taken as AD 793 (the date of the first recorded raid on the coastal monastery of Lindisfarne, in Northumbria), and its endpoint is 1066, with the battles of Fulford, Stamford Bridge and Hastings, which resulted in political conquest at the hands of the Normans. However, it should be understood that these dates are simply useful points of reference; the events in question had different impacts across the British Isles, and do not mark true watershed moments; life either side of 793, or of 1066 may not have felt very different. Moreover, no one living during this period thought of themselves as living in 'the Viking Age'. Nonetheless, such was the rate of social change through the period that the world of the late eighth century would have felt very alien to someone living in the mid-eleventh. For this reason, the term 'Viking Age' remains a useful label.

Wolin. A key centre of trade in the southern Baltic, particularly important from the tenth century onward.

York. Often thought of as the 'capital' of Viking England, some scholars have referred to the 'Viking Kingdom of York'. It is clear, based on both documentary and archaeological evidence, that York was one of the most important urban settlements of tenth- and eleventh-century England, and a focus for Scandinavian settlement and trade.

Bibliography

Äikäs, T., A.-K. Puputti, M. Núñez, J. Aspi & J. Okkonen 2009. 'Sacred and profane livelihood: animal bones from Sieidi sites in northern Finland', *Norwegian Archaeological Review* **42**(2): 109–122.

Abrams, L. 2012. 'Diaspora and identity in the Viking Age', *Early Medieval Europe* **20**: 17–38.

Aldhouse-Green, M. 2004a. 'Chaining and shaming: images of defeat, from Llyn Cerrig Bach to Sarmitzegetusa', *Oxford Journal of Archaeology* **23**(3): 319–340.

Aldhouse-Green, M. 2004b. 'Crowning glories: languages of hair in Later Prehistoric Europe', *Proceedings of The Prehistoric Society* **70**: 299–325.

Alexander, M. L. 1987. 'A Viking-Age grave from Cambois, Bedlington, Northumberland', *Medieval Archaeology* **31**: 101–105.

Almond, R. 2003. *Medieval Hunting*. Stroud, Sutton Publishing.

Ambrosiani, K. 1981. *Viking Age Combs, Comb Making and Comb Makers in the Light of Finds from Birka and Ribe*. Stockholm, Stockholm Studies in Archaeology 2.

Anderson, J. 1999. *The Orkneyinga Saga*. Edinburgh, Mercat Press.

Appadurai, A. (ed.) 1986. *The Social Life of Things: Commodities in Cultural Perspective*. Cambridge, Cambridge University Press.

Archer, J. 1946. *The Sikhs*. Princeton, Princeton University Press.

Aronsson, K.-Ã. 1991. *Forest Reindeer Herding AD 1–1800: Archaeology and Environment 10*. Umeå, University of Umeå.

Aronsson, K.-Ã. 1993. 'Comments on Sami Viking Age pastoralism – or "The Fur Trade Paradigm" reconsidered', *Norwegian Archaeological Review* **26**(1): 20–22.

Ashby, S. P. *in press-a*. 'Disentangling trade: combs in the North and Irish Seas in the Long Viking Age', in J. H. Barrett & S.-J. Gibbon (eds), *Maritime Societies of the Viking and Medieval World*.

Ashby, S. P. *in press-b*. 'Making a Good Comb: Mercantile Identity in 9th to 11th-century England', in L. Ten-Harkel & D. M. Hadley (eds), *Everyday Life in Viking Towns: Social Approaches to Towns in England and Ireland* c. *800–1100*. Oxford: Oxbow.

Ashby, S. P. *in prep*. 'Technologies of transformation: the agency of hair in early-medieval Europe'.

Ashby, S. P. 2002. 'The role of zooarchaeology in the interpretation of socioeconomic status: a discussion with reference to medieval Europe', *Archaeological Review from Cambridge* **18** (*Medieval Animals*, ed. A. Pluskowski): 37–59.

Ashby, S. P. 2006. *Time, Trade and Identity: Bone and Antler Combs in Northern Britain c. AD700–1400*. PhD thesis, University of York.

Ashby, S. P. 2006b. 'Trade in Viking Age Britain: Identity and the Production and Distribution of Bone and Antler Combs', in J. Arneborg. & B. Grønnow (eds), *Dynamics of Northern Societies. Proceedings of the SILA/NABO Conference on Arctic and North Atlantic Archaeology, Copenhagen, May 10th–14th, 2004*. Copenhagen: Publications from the National Museum, Studies in Archaeology and History Volume 10, 273–79.

Ashby, S. P. 2012. 'A Study in Regionality: Hair Combs and Bone/Antler Craft in North-east England *c*. AD 800–1100', in D. Petts & S. Turner (eds), *Early Medieval Northumbria: Kingdoms And Communities, AD 450–1100*. Turnhout: Brepols, 303–319.

Ashby, S. P. & A. Bolton 2010. 'Searching with a fine-toothed comb: Combs for Humans and Horses on the PAS database', in S. Worrell, G. Egan, J. Naylor, K. Leahy & M. J. Lewis (eds), *A Decade of Discovery: Proceedings of the Portable Antiquities Scheme Conference 2007* (British Archaeological Reports, British Series 520). Oxford, Archaeopress.

Asleson, M. A., E. C. Hellgren & L. W. Varner 1996. 'Nitrogen requirements for antler growth and maintenance in white-tailed deer', *Journal of Wildlife Management* **60**(4): 744–752.

Asleson, M. A., E. C. Hellgren & L. W. Varner 1997. 'Effects of seasonal protein restriction on antlerogenesis and body mass in adult male white-tailed deer', *Journal of Wildlife Management* **61**(4): 1098–1107.

Azorit, C., M. Analla, R. Carrasco & J. Munoz-Cobo 2002. 'Influence of age and environment on antler traits in Spanish red deer (*Cervus elaphus hispanicus*)', *Zeitschrift Fur Jagdwissenschaft* **48**(3): 137–144.

Baker, P. S. 2000. *The Anglo-Saxon Chronicle: A Collaborative Edition Volume 8*. Cambridge, D. S. Brewer.

Barrett, J. H. 2008. 'The Norse in Scotland' in S. Brink & N. S. Price (eds), *The Viking World*. London: Routledge, 411–427.

Barth, E. K.1983. 'Trapping reindeer in South Norway', *Antiquity* 57 (**220**): 109–115.

Bartlett, R. 1994. 'Symbolic meanings of hair in the Middle Ages', *Transactions of the Royal Historical Society, sixth series* 4: 43–60.

Bartman, E. 2001. 'Hair and the artifice of Roman female adornment', *American Journal of Archaeology* **105**(1): 1–25.

Bath, M. 1992. *The Image of the Stag: Iconographic themes in Western Art, Saecula spiritalia, Vol. 24.* Baden Baden: V. Koerner.

Battiscombe, C. F. (ed.) 1956. *The Relics of Saint Cuthbert.* Oxford, Oxford University Press.

Berg, C. 1951. *The Unconscious Significance of Hair.* London, George Allen & Unwin.

Bergman, I., L. Östlund, O. Azckrisson & L. Liedgren 2007. 'Stones in the snow: A Norse fur traders' road in Sami country', *Antiquity* **81**: 397–408.

Bickle, P. 2007. 'I'm your Venus: making surfaces on the body', in J. Thomas (ed.), *Overcoming the Modern Invention of Material Culture: Proceedings of the Tag Session, Exeter 2006.* Porto, ADECAP: 257–270.

Bijker, W. E. & J. Law (eds) 1994. *Shaping Technology/Building Society: Studies in Sociotechnical Change.* Cambridge, MA: MIT Press.

Blehr, O. 1973. 'Traditional Reindeer Hunting and Social Change in the Local Communities Surrounding Hardangervidda', *Norwegian Archaeological Review* 6: 102–112.

Bradley, R. (ed.) 2000. *An Archaeology of Natural Places.* London, Routledge.

Bradley, R. & M. Edmonds 2005. *Interpreting the Axe Trade: Production and Exchange in Neolithic Britain (New Studies in Archaeology).* Cambridge, Cambridge University Press.

Brett, G. 1956. 'The 'Rider' Silks', in C. F. Battiscomb (ed.), *The Relics of Saint Cuthbert.* Oxford: Oxford University Press, 470–483.

Brothwell, D. R. 1976. 'Further evidence of bone chewing by ungulates: the sheep of North Ronaldsay, Orkney', *Journal of Archaeological Science* 3: 179–182.

Bubenik, G. A. 1990. 'Neuroendocrine Regulation of the Antler Cycle', in G. A. Bubenik & A. B. Bubenik (eds), *Horns, Pronghorns, and Antlers.* New York: Springer-Verlag, 265–297.

Bubenik, G. A. & A. B. Bubenik (eds) 1990. *Horns, Pronghorns, and Antlers.* New York: Springer-Verlag.

Buckland, T. 1980. 'The Reindeer Antlers of the Abbots Bromley Horn Dance: a re-examination', *Lore and Language* 3(2): 1–8.

Burch, E. S. 1972. 'The caribou/wild reindeer as a human resource', *American Antiquity* 37(3): 339–367.

Callmer, J. 1998. 'Archaeological Sources for the Presence of Frisian Agents of Trade in Northern Europe *ca*. AD 700–900', in A. Wesse (ed.), *Studien zur Archäologie des Ostseeraumes von der Eisenzeit Mittelalter. Festschrift für Michael Müller-Wille*. Neumünster, Wachholtz Verlag: 469–481.

Callmer, J. 2002. 'North-European trading centres and the Early Medieval craftsman: Craftsmen at Åhus, north-eastern Scania, Sweden ca. AD 750–850', in Hårdh, B. & L. Larsson (eds), *Central Places in the Migration and the Merovingian periods*. Stockholm: Almqvist & Wiksell, 125–157.

Callmer, J. 2003. 'Wayland: An Essay on Craft Production in the Early and High Middle Ages in Scandinavia', in L. Larsson & B. Hårdh (eds), *Centrality – Regionality: The Social Structure of Southern Sweden during the Iron Age. Uppåkrastudier 7. Acta Archaeologica Lundensia Ser. 8 no. 40.* Lund: Almqvist & Wiksell, 337–361.

Callow, C. 2006. 'Reconstructing the past in medieval Iceland', *Early Medieval Europe* 4(3): 297–324.

Cameron, E. (ed.) 1998. *Leather and Fur: Aspects of Early Medieval Trade and Technology*. London, Archetype Publications.

Carpelan, C. 1993. 'Comments on Sami Viking Age pastoralism – or "The Fur Trade Paradigm" reconsidered', *Norwegian Archaeological Review* 26(1): 22–26.

Carver, M. O. H. 1990. 'Pre-Viking Traffic in the North Sea', in S. Mcgrail (ed.), *Maritime Celts, Frisians and Saxons, CBA Research Report 71.* London, Council for British Archaeology.

Chapman, D. I. 1975. 'Antlers – bones of contention', *Mammal Review* 5(4): 121–172.

Chapman, D. I. 1981. 'Antler structure and function – a hypothesis', *Journal of Biomechanics* 14 (3): 195–197.

Christensen, A. E. 1987. 'Reindeer-hunter and comb-maker – A combination of trades in the Iron Age', *Tools and Trades* 4: 11–32.

Christophersen, A. 1980. 'Raw material, resources and production capacity in early medieval comb manufacture in Lund', *Meddelanden Fran Lunds Universitets Historiska Museum*, NYA SE Part, 150–165.

Clarke, D. & A. Heald 2002. 'Beyond typology: combs, economics, symbolism and regional identity in Late Norse Scotland', *Norwegian Archaeological Review* 35(2): 81–93.

Cleland, L., M. Harlow & L. Llewellyn-Jones (eds) 2005. *The Clothed Body in the Ancient World*. Oxford, Oxbow.

Cnotliwy, E. 1956. 'Z badan nad rzemioslem zajmujacym sie obróbka rogi i kosci na Pomorzu Zachonim we wczesnym sredniowieczu', *Materialy Zachodnio-Pomorskie*, **2**: 151–179.

Cnotliwy, E. 1973. *Rzemiosło Rogownicze na Pomorzu Sczesnośredniowiecznym (Antler Handicraft in Early Medieval Pomerania)*. Wroclaw, Polska Akademia Nauk Instytut Historii Kultury Materialnej.

Conneller, C. 2004. 'Becoming deer: corporeal transformations at Star Carr', *Archaeological Dialogues* **11**: 37–56.

Conneller, C. 2011. *An Archaeology of Materials: Substantial Transformations in Early Prehistoric Europe*. London, Routledge.

Cook, R. (trans.) 2001. *Njal's Saga*. London, Penguin.

Cummins, J. 1988. *The Hound and the Hawk: the Art of Medieval Hunting*. London, Weidenfeld & Nicolson.

Cummins, W. A. 1999. *The Picts and Their Symbols*. Stroud, Sutton.

Davidson, H. R. E. & P. Fisher (trans.) 1980. *Saxo Grammaticus: The History of the Danes (Books I-IX)*. Cambridge, Brewer.

Derks, T. & W. Vos 2010. 'Wooden combs from the Roman fort at Vechten: the bodily appearance of soldiers', *Journal of Archaeology in the Low Countries* **2**(2): 53–77.

Derrett, J. D. M. 1973. 'Religious hair', *Man* **8**: 100–103.

Dobres, M.-A. 2000. *Technology and Social Agency*. Oxford, Blackwell.

Douglas, M. 1966. *Purity and Danger: An Analysis of Concepts of Pollution and Taboo*. London, Routledge & Kegan Paul.

Drew, J. H. 1965. 'The horn comb industry of Kenilworth', *Transactions and Proceedings of the Birmingham Archaeological Society* **82**: 21–7.

DuBois, T. A. 1999. *Nordic Religions in the Viking Age*. Philadelphia, University of Pennsylvania Press.

Dunbar, R. 1998. *Grooming, Gossip, and the Evolution of Language*. Cambridge, MA: Harvard University Press.

Dunlevy, M. M. 1988. 'A classification of early Irish combs', *Proceedings of the Royal Irish Academy* **88**(C11): 341–422.

Dutton, P. E. 2004. 'Charlemagne's Mustache', in P. E. Dutton, *Charlemagne's Mustache and Other Cultural Clusters of a Dark Age*. New York: Palgrave MacMillan, 3–42.

Eckardt, H. & N. Crummy. 2008. *Styling the body in Late Iron Age and Roman Britain: a contextual approach to toilet instruments. Instrumentum Monograph 36*. Montagnac, Instrumentum.

Edmonds, M. 1995. *Stone Tools and Society: Working Stone in Neolithic and Bronze Age Britain*. London, Batsford.

Edmonds, M. 1999. *Ancestral Geographies of the Neolithic. Landscapes, monuments and memory*. London, Routledge.

Edmonds, M. 2004. *The Langdales. Landscape and Prehistory in a Lakeland Valley*. Stroud, Tempus.

Eldjárn, K. (ed.) 2000. *Kuml og Haugfé úr Heidnum sid á Íslandi* (2nd edition, revised and edited by Adolf Fridriksson). Reykjavík, Mál og menning.

European Commission: Raphael Programme 1998. *The Normans, a European People*. [Accessed 20 August 2004. Available from: http://www.mondes-normands.caen.fr/angleterre/archeo/Angleterre/bone/comb.htm.]

Faulkes, A. (trans.) 2002. *Snorri Sturluson, 'Edda'*. Vermont and London, Everyman (Dent & Tuttle).

Fischer Drew, K. (trans.) 1949. *The Burgundian Code*. Philadelphia, University of Pennsylvania Press.

Fisher, P.(trans.) 1979. *Saxo Grammaticus, The History of the Danes*. Woodbridge, Suffolk: Boydell & Brewer.

Flanagan, J. F. 1956. 'The Figured Silks', in C. F. Battiscombe (ed.), *The Relics of Saint Cuthbert*. Oxford: Oxford University Press, 484–525.

Fletcher, J. 2000. 'Hair', in P. Nicholson & I. Shaw (eds), *Ancient Egyptian Materials and Technology*, Cambridge: Cambridge University Press, 495–501.

Fletcher, J. 2005. 'The Decorated Body in Ancient Egypt: hairstyles, cosmetics and tattoos', in L. Cleland, M. Harlow, & L. Llewellyn-Jones (eds), *The Clothed Body in the Ancient World*. Oxford: Oxbow, 3–13.

Flodin, L. 1989. *Kammakerieti i Trodheim ca. 1000–1600. Folkebibliotekstomten Meddelselser nr 14*. Trondheim: Riksantikvarien, Fortiden i Trondheim bygrunn.

Foster, S. M. 1990. 'Pins, Combs and the Chronology of Later Iron Age Settlement', in I. Armit (ed.), *Beyond the Brochs: Changing Perspectives on the Later Iron Age in Atlantic Scotland*. Edinburgh: Edinburgh University Press, 143–174.

Frazer, J. G. 1913. *The Golden Bough: A Study in Magic and Religion*. London, MacMillan.

Fry, T. (trans.) 1981. *The Rule of St Benedict in Latin and English with notes*. Collegeville, MN: Liturgical Press.

Galloway, P. & M. Newcomer 1981. 'The craft of comb-making: An experimental enquiry', *University of London Institute of Archaeology Bulletin* 18: 73–90.

Gansum, T. 1993. 'Hår og stil of stilig hår: Om langhåret maktsymbolikk', in Rolfsen, P. & F. A. Stylegar (eds), *Smartemofunnene i Nytt Lys*. Oslo: University of Oslo, 191–221.

Gell, A. 1992. 'The Technology of Enchantment and the Enchantment of Technology', in J. Coote & A. Shelton (eds), *Anthropology, Art and Aesthetics*. Oxford, Clarendon.

Geselowitz, M. N. 1993. 'Archaeology and the Social Study of Technological Innovation', *Science, Technology, & Human Values* **18**(2): 231–246.

Gibson, J. & F. Bradford 2008. *Rising Tides: The Loss of Coastal Heritage in Orkney*. Orkney, Northings.

Gibson, J. J. 1979. *The Ecological Approach to Visual Perception*. Boston, Houghton Mifflin.

Gilchrist, R. 2012. *Medieval Life: Archaeology and the Life Course*. Boydell & Brewer, Woodbridge.

Goosmann, E. 2012. 'The long-haired kings of the Franks: "like so many Samsons?"', *Early Medieval Europe* **20**: 233–259.

Goss, R. J. 1969. 'Photoperiodic control of antler cycles in deer.1: phase shift and frequency changes', *Journal of Experimental Zoology* **170**: 311–324.

Goss, R. J. 1995. 'Future directions in antler research', *Anatomical Record* **241**(3): 291–302.

Gourevitch, P. 1999. *We wish to inform you that tomorrow we will be killed with our families*. London, Picador.

Graham-Campbell, J. 1985. 'A lost Pictish treasure (and two Viking-age gold arm-rings) from the Broch of Burgar, Orkney', *Proceedings of the Society of Antiquaries of Scotland* **115**: 241–261.

Graham-Campbell, J. & C. E. Batey 1998. *Vikings in Scotland: An Archaeological Survey*. Edinburgh, Edinburgh University Press.

Green, M. J. 1992. *Animals in Celtic Life and Myth*. London, Routledge.

Haigh, D. H. 1871. 'Yorkshire Runic Monuments', *Yorkshire Archaeological Journal* **2**: 253–288.

Hall, R. A. & M. Whyman 1996. 'Settlement and monasticism at Ripon, North Yorkshire, from the 7th to the 11th centuries AD', *Medieval Archaeology* **40**: 62–150.

Hall, T. 1654. *Comarum akosmia: the loathsomenesse of long haire, or, A treatise wherein you have the question stated, many arguments against it produc'd, and the most materiall arguguments [sic] for it refell'd and answer'd : with the concurrent judgement of divines both old and new against it, with an appendix against painting, spots, naked breasts (etc)*. London, Nathanael Webb & William Grantham.

Hallpike, C. R. 1969. 'Social Hair', *Man* **4**: 256–264. Also published as Hallpike, C. R. 1979. 'Social Hair', in W. A. Lessa & E. Z. Vogt (eds), *Reader in Comparative Religion: An Anthropological Approach*. New York: Harper & Row, 99–105.

Hambleton, E. & P. Rowley-Conwy 1997. 'The Medieval Reindeer Economy at Gæccevaj'njar'ga 244B in the Varanger Fjord, North Norway', *Norwegian Archaeological Review* **30**(1): 55–70.

Hamilakis, Y., M. Pluciennik & S. Tarlow (eds) 2002. *Thinking through the Body: Archaeologies of Corporeality*. New York, Kluwer Academic/Plenum Publishers.

Hansen, G. 2005. *Bergen c. 800–1170: The Emergence of a Town*. Bergen: Fagbokforlaget, The Bryggen Papers Main Series No. 6.

Hansen, L. I. 1993. 'Comments on Sami Viking Age pastoralism – or "The Fur Trade Paradigm" reconsidered', *Norwegian Archaeological Review* **26**(1): 34–40.

Hassig, D. 1995. *Medieval Bestiaries: Text, Image, Ideology*. Cambridge, Cambridge University Press.

Heikura, K., E. Pulliainen, P. Danilov, E. Erkinaro, V. Markovsky, L. Bljudnik, S. Sulkava & E. Lindgren 1985. 'Wild forest reindeer, Rangifer tarandus fennicus Loennb., its historical and recent occurrence and distribution in Finland and the Karelian ASSR (USSR) with special reference to the development and movements of the Kuhmo (Finland) – Kamennojeozero (USSR) subpopulation', *Aquilo Ser. Zoologica* **23**: 22–45.

Hershman, P. 1974. 'Hair, sex, and dirt', *Man* **9**(2): 274–298.

Hicks, C. 1993. *Animals in Early Medieval Art*. Edinburgh, Edinburgh University Press.

Hielscher, S. 2011. *Are you worth it? A Practice-Orientated Approach to Everyday Hair Care to Inform Sustainable Design and Sustainable Consumption Strategies*. PhD Thesis, Nottingham Trent University.

Higgitt, J. 1987. 'The Jedburgh Comb', in N. Stratford (ed.), *Romanesque and Gothic: Essays for George Zarnecki*. Wolfeboro, NH: Boydell, 118–127.

Higgitt, J. 1995. 'The Comb, Pendant and Buckle', in J. H. Lewis & G. J. Ewart (eds), *Jedburgh Abbey: the Archaeology and Architecture of a Border Abbey. SAS Monograph 10*. Edinburgh, Society of Antiquaries of Scotland.

Hiltebeitel, A. 1998. 'Introduction: Hair Tropes', in A. Hiltebeitel & B. D. Miller (eds), *Hair: its Power and Meaning in Asian Cultures*. Albany, NY: State University of New York Press, 1–9.

Hodgson, C. 1832. 'An account of some antiquities found in a cairn, near Hesket-in-the-Forest in Cumberland', *Archaeologia Aeliana* **2**: 106–109.

Hollander, L. M. (trans.) 1949. *The Sagas of Kormák and The Sworn Brothers*. Princeton, Princeton University Press.

Hollander, L. M.(trans.) 1995. *Heimskringla: History of the Kings of Norway, by Snorri Sturluson*. Austin: University of Texas Press.

Holmquist Olausson, L. 1990. '"Älgmannen" från Birka. Presentation av en nyligen undersökt krigargrav med människooffer', *Fornvannen* 85: 175–182.

Hoskins, J. 1998. *Biographical Objects*. London, Routledge.

Hudson-Edwards, K. A., M. G. Macklin, R. Finlayson & D. G. Passmore 1999a. 'Medieval lead pollution in the River Ouse at York, England', *Journal of Archaeological Science* 26: 809–819.

Hudson-Edwards, K. A., M. G. Macklin & M. P. Taylor 1999b. '2000 years of sediment-borne heavy metal storage in the Yorkshire Ouse basin, NE England', *Hydrological Processes* 13: 1087–1102.

Hughes, T. P. 1994. 'Technological Momentum', in L. Marx & M. Roe Smith (eds), *Does Technology Drive History? The Dilemma of Technological Determinism*. Cambridge, MA: MIT Press.

Hultkrantz, Ã. K. 1985. 'Reindeer nomadism and the religion of the Saamis', *Arv. Scandinavian Yearbook of Folklore (later Arv. Nordic Yearbook of Folklore)* **39 for 1983**: Nov. 28.

Huxley, J. S. 1926. 'The annual increment of the antlers of the red deer (*Cervus elaphus*)', *Proceedings of the Zoological Society of London* 96(4): 1021–1035.

Huxley, J. S. 1931. 'The relative size of antlers in deer', *Proceedings of the Zoological Society of London* 101(3): 819–864.

Indrelid, S. & A. K. Hufthammer 2011. 'Medieval mass trapping of reindeer at the Hardangervidda mountain plateau, South Norway', *Quaternary International* 238(1–2): 44–54.

Ingold, T. 1980. *Hunters, Pastoralists and Ranchers: Reindeer Economies and their Transformations*. Cambridge, Cambridge University Press.

Ingold, T. 1993. 'The Reindeerman's Lasso', in P. Lemonnier (ed.), *Technological Choices: Transformation in Material Cultures since the Neolithic*. London: Routledge, 108–125.

Ingold, T. 2000. *The Perception of the Environment*. London, Routledge.

Ingold, T. 2011. *Being Alive: Essays on Movement, Knowledge, and Desciption*. London, Routledge.

Ingram, J. 1912. *The Anglo-Saxon Chronicle*. London, J. M. Dent & Sons.

Jackson, L. J. & P. T. Thacker (eds) 1997. *Caribou and Reindeer Hunters of the Northern Hemisphere (Worldwide Archaeology Series)*. Aldershot, Avebury: Ashgate Publishing.

James, E. 1988. *The Franks*. Oxford, Blackwell.

Jones, C. A. 1998. *Aelfric's Letter to the Monks of Eynsham*. Cambridge, Cambridge University Press.

Jones, G. & T. J. Jones (trans.) 1949. *The Mabinogion*. London, Dent.

Jordhøy, P. 2008. 'Ancient wild reindeer pitfall trapping systems as indicators for former migration patterns and habitat use in the Dovre region, southern Norway', *Rangifer* **28**(1): 79–87.

Joy, J. 2010. *Iron Age Mirrors: A Biographical Approach. British Archaeological Reports British Series 518.* Oxford, Archaeopress.

Joyce, R. A. 2005. 'Archaeology of the body', *Annual Review of Anthropology* **34**: 139–158.

Kaland, S. H. H. 1993. 'The Settlement of Westness, Rousay', in C. E. Batey, J. Jesch & C. D. M. Morris (eds), *The Viking Age in Caithness, Orkney and the North Atlantic: Select Papers from the Proceedings of the Eleventh Viking Congress, Thurso and Kirkwall, 22 August – 1 September 1989.* Edinburgh, Edinburgh University Press.

Keynes, S. & M. Lapidge (eds) 1983. *Alfred the Great: Asser's Life of King Alfred and Other Contemporary Sources.* London, Penguin.

Kierdorf, U., H. Kierdorf & A. Boyde 2000. 'Structure and mineralisation density of antler and pedicle bone in red deer (*Cervus elaphus* L.) exposed to different levels of environmental fluoride: a quanitative backscattered electron imaging study', *Journal of Anatomy* **196**: 71–83.

Kierdorf, U., H. Kierdorf & S. Knuth 1995. 'Effects of castration on antler growth in fallow deer (*Dama dama* L.)', *Journal of Experimental Zoology* **273**: 33–43.

Kitchener, A. C. 2010. 'The Elk', in T. P. O'Connor & N. Sykes (eds), *Extinctions and Invasions: A Social History of British Fauna.* Oxford: Windgather Press, 36–42.

Kitzinger, E. 1956. 'The Coffin-Reliquary' in C. F. Battiscombe (ed.), *The Relics of Saint Cuthbert*, Oxford: Oxford University Press, 202–304.

Kohn, M. & S. Mithen 1999. 'Handaxes: products of sexual selection?', *Antiquity* **73**: 518–526.

Kopytoff, I. 1986. 'The Cultural Biography of Things: Commoditization as Process', in A. Appadurai (ed.) *The Social Life of Things; Commodities in Cultural Perspective.* Cambridge: Cambridge University Press, 64–91.

Laing, S. (trans.) & E. Rhys (ed.) 1930. *Heimskringla: The Norse King Sagas by Snorre Sturrlason.* London: Jim Dent & Sons.

Lasko, P. 1956. 'The Comb of St. Cuthbert' in C. F. Battiscombe (ed.), *The Relics of Saint Cuthbert.* Oxford, Oxford University Press.

Leach, E. R. 1958. 'Magical hair', *Journal of the Royal Anthropological Institute of Great Britain and Ireland* **88**(2): 147–164.

Lemonnier, P. (ed.) 1993. *Technological Choices: Transformation in Material Cultures since the Neolithic.* London, Routledge.

Li, C., D. E. Clark & J. M. Suttie 2003. 'Deer Pedicle Height, Tissue Interactions and Antler Evolution', *Deer* **12**(6): 333–338.

Lincoln, G. A. 1992. 'Biology of Antlers', *Journal of Zoology* **226**: 517–528.

Lincoln, G. & T. Fletcher 1984. 'History of a Hummel Part VII: Nature vs. Nurture', *Deer* **6**: 127–131.

Lyasight, A. M. 1971. 'Note on a grave excavated by Joseph Banks and Geoge Low at Skaill in 1772', *Proceedings of the Society of Antiquaries of Scotland* **104**: 285–289.

MacEwen, W. 1920. *The Growth and Shedding of the Antler of the Deer: The Histological Phenomena and their Relation to the Growth of Bone.* Glasgow: Maclehose, Jackson & Co.

Macgregor, A. 1985. *Bone, Antler, Ivory and Horn: The Technology of Skeletal Materials Since the Roman Period.* London, Croom Helm.

MacGregor, A., A. J. Mainman & N. S. H. Rogers (eds) 1999. *Craft, Industry and Everyday Life: Bone, Antler, Ivory and Horn from Anglo-Scandinavian and Medieval York. The Archaeology of York 17/2.* York, Council for British Archaeology.

MacGregor, A. & J. D. Currey (1983). 'Mechanical properties as conditioning factors in the bone and antler industry of the 3rd to the 13th Century AD', *Journal of Archaeological Science* **10**: 71–77.

MacGregor, N. 2010. *A History of the World in 100 Objects.* London: Allan Lane, Penguin.

McIntyre, J. 1929. 'Anglian Comb from Whitby', *Yorkshire Archaeological Journal* **29**(116): 350.

Magnus, O. 1555. *Historia de Gentibus Septentrionalibus.* Rome, de Viottis.

Magnusson, M. & H. Pálsson (trans) 1960. *Njal's Saga.* London, Penguin.

Mann, J. E. 1982. *Early Medieval Finds from Flaxengate, 1: Objects of Antler, Bone, Stone, Horn, Ivory, Amber, and Jet.* London, Council for British Archaeology.

Mason, C. 2008. 'Secrets of the shed masters', *Outdoor Life* **March 08**: 36–40.

Meaney, A. L. 1981. *Anglo-Saxon Amulets and Curing Stones. British Archaeological Reports British Series 96.* Oxford, John & Erica Hedges.

Merleau-Ponty, M. 1962. *Phenomenology of Perception.* London, Routledge & Kegan Paul.

Meyer, K. (ed. & trans.) 1906. *The Triads of Ireland. Todd Lecture Series 13.* Dublin, Royal Irish Academy.

Miller, B. D. 1998. 'Afterword: Hair Power', in A. Hiltebeitel & B. D. Miller (eds), *Hair: its Power and Meaning in Asian Cultures.* Albany, NY: State University of New York Press, 281–286.

Miller, D. 2002. 'Artefacts and the meaning of things', in T. Ingold (ed.), *Companion Encyclopedia of Anthropology*. London: Routledge, 396–419.

Miller, D. (ed.) 2005. *Material Cultures: Why some things matter.* Chicago, University of Chicago Press.

Miller, D. (ed.) 2008. *The Comfort of Things*. Cambridge, Polity Press.

Mitchell, B., B. W. Staines & D. Welch 1977. *Ecology of Red Deer: A Research Review Relevant to their Management in Scotland.* Cambridge, Institute of Terrestrial Ecology.

Morris, C. D. M. 1996. *The Birsay Bay project Volume 1: Coastal Sites beside the Brough Road, Birsay, Orkney Excavations 1976–1982.* Durham, University of Durham.

Morris, W. & E. Magnússon 1894. *The Saga Library volume IV: The Stories of the Kings of Norway called the Round World (Heimskringla) by Snorri Sturluson.* London, Bernard Quarith.

Muir, P. D. & A. R. Sykes 1988. 'Effect of winter nutrition on antler development in red deer (*Cervus elaphus*) – a field study', *New Zealand Journal of Agricultural Research* 31(2): 145–150.

Mulk, I.-M. 1993. 'Comments on Sami Viking Age pastoralism – or "The Fur Trade Paradigm" reconsidered', *Norwegian Archaeological Review* 26(1): 28–34.

Mumcuoglu, K. Y. & J. Zias 1989. 'How the Ancients De-loused Themselves', *Biblical Archaeology Review* 15(6): 66–69.

Nicholson, A. 1997. 'The Antler', in P. Hill (ed.), *Whithorn and St Ninian: The Excavation of a Monastic Town, 1984–91.* Stroud: Sutton, 474–495.

Obeyesekere, G. 1981. *Medusa's Hair: An Essay on Personal Symbols and Religious Experience*. Chicago, University of Chicago Press.

Odner, K. 1985. 'Saamis (Lapps), Finns and Scandinavians in History and Prehistory. Ethnic Origins and Ethnic Processes in Fenno-Scandinavia', *Norwegian Archaeological Review* 18(1–2): 1–13.

Odner, K. 1992. *The Varanger Saami: Habitation and Economy AD 1200–1900.* Oslo, Scandinavian University Press.

Odner, K. 1993. 'Comments on Sami Viking Age pastoralism – or "The Fur Trade Paradigm" reconsidered', *Norwegian Archaeological Review* 26(1): 26–28.

Okasha, E. 1999. 'An Inscribed Bone Fragment from Nassington, Peterborough', *Medieval Archaeology* 43: 203–205.

Olivelle, P. 1998. 'Hair and Society: Social Significance of Hair in South Asian Traditions', in A. Hiltebeitel & B. D. Miller (eds), *Hair: its Power and Meaning in Asian Cultures*. Albany, NY: State University of New York Press, 11–49.

Olsen, B. 1985. 'Comments on Saamis, Finns and Scandinavians in History and Prehistory', *Norwegian Archaeological Review* **18**(1–2): 13–18.

Olsen, B. 2003. 'Belligerent Chieftains and Oppressed Hunters? Changing Conceptions of Interethnic Relationships in Northern Norway during the Iron Age and the Early Medieval Period', in J. H. Barrett (ed.), *Contact, Continuity, and Collapse: The Norse Colonisation of the North Atlantic*. Turnhout: Brepols, 9–31.

Owen, O. & M. Dalland (eds) 1999. *Scar: A Viking Boat Burial on Sanday, Orkney*. Phantassie, Scotland: Tuckwell Press.

Paine, R. 1988. 'Reindeer and caribou *Rangifer tarandus* in the wild and under pastoralism', *Polar Record* **24**: 31–42.

Pálsson, H. & P. Edwards (eds) 1972. *Erbyggja Saga*. London, Penguin.

Paterson, H. 2012. *Power and Possession: The Importance of Dress and Personal Adornment to the Construction of Complex Societies in Early Medieval Northern Britain and Ireland*. Unpublished PhD thesis, Department of Archaeology, University of York.

Pinch, T. & Bijker, W. E. 1987. 'The Social Construction of Facts and Artifacts: Or How the Sociology of Science and the Sociology of Technology Might Benefit Each Other', in W. E. Bijker, T. P. Hughes & T. Pinch (eds) *The Social Construction of Technological System*. Cambridge: MIT Press, 17–50.

Pohl, W. 1998. 'Telling the difference: Signs of ethnic identity', in W. Pohl & H. Reimitz (eds), *Strategies of Distinction: The Construction of Ethnic Communities, 300–800*. Leiden: Brill, 17–69.

Polanyi, M. 1967. *The Tacit Dimension*. Garden City, NY: Anchor Books.

Price, N. S. 2002. *The Viking Way: Religion and War in Late Iron Age Scandinavia*. Uppsala, Uppsala University Department of Archaeology & Ancient History.

Price, N. S. 2010. 'Passing into Poetry: Viking Age Mortuary Drama and the Origins of Norse Mythology', *Medieval Archaeology* **54**: 123–157.

Rackham, H. 1940. *Pliny: 'Natural History', with an English Translation in Ten Volumes. Volume III: Libri VIII-XI. The Loeb Classical Library*. Cambrdge, MA: Harvard University Press.

Radford, C. A. R. 1959. *The Early Christian and Norse Settlements, Birsay*. Edinburgh, HMSO.

Rankama, T. & P. Ukkonen 2001. 'On the early history of the wild reindeer in Finland', *Boreas* **30**(2): 131–147.

Reichstein, H. 1969. 'Untersuchungen von geweihresten des Rothirsches (*Cervus elpahus* L.) aus der frühmittelalterlichen Siedlung Haithabu (Ausgrabung 1963–64)', in K. Schietzel (ed.), *Berichte über die Ausgrabungen in Haithabu 2*. Neumünster: Karl Wachholtz Verlag, 57–71.

Reischer, E. & K. S. Koo 2004. 'The body beautiful: symbolism and agency in the social world', *Annual Review of Anthropology* **33**: 297–317.

Ribeiro, E. 1986. *Dress and Morality*. New York, Holmes & Meier.

Riddler, I. 1990. 'Saxon Handled Combs from London', *Transactions of the London and Middlesex Archaeological Society* **41**: 9–20.

Riddler, I. 1998. 'Combs with Perforated Handles', *The Archaeology of Canterbury* **8**: 189–198.

Robins, G. 1999. 'Hair and the construction of identity in Ancient Egypt, *c*. 1480–1350 B.C.', *Journal of the American Research Center in Egypt* **36**: 55–69.

Rydh, H. 1936. *Förhistoriska undersökningar på Adelsö*. Stockholm, KVHAA.

Rytter, J. 2001. 'Håndverk i Middelalderens Konghelle', in H. Andersson, K. Carlsson & M. Vretemark (eds), *Kungahälla: Problem och forskning kring stadens äldsta historia (Kungahälla: Problems and research on the early history of the town)*. Lund Studies in Medieval Archaeology Nr 28. Stockholm and Uddevalla: Almqvist & Wiksell, 75–110.

Said, E. W. 1978. *Orientalism*. London, Routledge & Kegan Paul.

Salmi, A.-K., T. Äikäs & S. Lipkin 2011. 'Animating rituals at Sámi sacred sites in northern Finland', *Journal of Social Archaeology* **11**(2): 212–235.

Salvesen, S. 1929. 'The Moose and Red Deer in Norway', *Journal of Mammalogy* **10**: 59–62.

Schama, S. 2010. *Scribble, Scribble, Scribble: Writing on Politics, Ice Cream, Churchill, and My Mother*. London, Bodley Head.

Schelvis, J. 1994. 'Caught between the teeth. A review of Dutch finds of archaeological remains of ectoparasites in combs', in M. J. Sommeijer & J. van der Blom (eds), *Experimental and Applied Entomology (Proceedings of the Netherlands Entomological Society* **5**: 131–132.

Schildkrout, E. 2004. 'Inscribing the Body', *Annual Review of Anthropology* **33**: 319–344.

Schmidt, K. T., A. Stien, S. D. Albon & F. E. Guinness 2001. 'Antler Length of Yearling Red Deer is Determined By Population Density, Weather and Early Life History', *Oecologia* **127**: 191–197.

Sharples, N. 2003. 'From Monuments to Artefacts: Changing Social Relationships in the Later Iron Age', in J. Downes & A. Ritchie (eds), *Sea Change: Orkney and Northern Europe in the Later Iron Age AD 300–800*. Balgavies, Forfar, Angus: Pinkfoot Press & Orkney Heritage Society, 151–165.

Shawcross, W. S. 1964. 'An archaeological assemblage of Maori combs', *Journal of the Polynesian Society* **73**: 382–398.

Sheppard, T. 1904. 'Ancient Russian ornaments and weapons', *The Antiquary* 50: 50–54.

Sherley-Price, L. 1990. *Bede, 'Ecclesiastical History of the English People'*. London, Penguin.

Shove, E. 2003. *Comfort, Cleanliness and Convenience. The Social Organization of Normality*. Oxford, Berg.

Sigurðson, J. V. 2007. 'The Appearance and Personal Abilities of Goðar, Jarlar, and Konungar: Iceland, Orkney, and Norway', in B. Ballin Smith, S. Taylor, & G. Williams (eds), *West Over Sea: Studies in Scandinavian Sea-Borne Expansion and Settlement Before 1300*. Leiden: Brill, 95–109.

Sinclair, A. & N. Schlanger (eds) 1990. *Technology in the Humanities: Archaeological Review from Cambridge 9:1*. Cambridge, University of Cambridge.

Sindbaek, S. M. 2007a. 'Networks and nodal points: the emergence of towns in early Viking Age Scandinavia', *Antiquity* 81: 119–132.

Sindbaek, S. M. 2007b. 'The Small World of the Vikings: Networks in Early Medieval Communication and Exchange', *Norwegian Archaeological Review* 40(1): 59–74.

Sindbaek, S. M. 2008. 'The Lands of Denemearce: Cultural Differences and Social Networks of the Viking Age in South Scandinavia', *Viking and Medieval Scandinavia* 4: 169–208.

Sindbaek, S. M. 2011, 'Silver Economies and Social Ties: Long-Distance Interaction, Long-Term Investments – and why the Viking Age happened', in J. Graham-Campbell, S. M. Sindbaek, & G. Williams (eds), *Silver Economies, Monetisation and Society in Scandinavia AD 800–1100*. Moesgård: Aarhus University Press, 41–66.

Singh, R. K. 1998. 'The significance of male hair: its presence and removal', *The Backlash!* [Accessed 28 May 2005. Available from: http://www.choisser.com/longhair/rajsingh.html]

Smiley, J. (ed.) 2000. *The Sagas of Icelanders*. New York, Viking (Penguin Group).

Smirnova, L. 1997. 'Antler, Bone and Ivory Working in Nerevsky and Lyudin Ends of Medieval Novgorod: Evidence from Waste Analysis', in G. De Boe & F. Verhaeghe (eds), *Material Culture in Medieval Europe: Papers of the 'Medieval Europe Brugge 1997' Conference, IAP Rapporten 07*. Zellik: Medieval Europe 1997, 137–146.

Smirnova, L. 2005. *Comb-Making in Medieval Novgorod (950–1450): An industry in transition. British Archaeological Reports International Series 1369*. Oxford, Archaeopress.

Smith, A. N. 2003. 'From the Small Green Isles to the Low Countries: Artefactual Evidence for Contact Around the North Sea Basin in the

Later Iron Age', in J. Downes & A. Ritchie (eds), *Sea Change: Orkney and Northern Europe in the Later Iron Age AD 300–800*. Balgavies, Forfar, Angus: Pinkfoot Press & Orkney Heritage Society, 111–116.

Smyser, H. M. 1965. 'Ibn Fadlan's Account of the Rus with Some Allusions to Beowulf', in J. B. Bessinger & R. P. Creed (eds), *Franciplegius: Medieval and Linguistic Studies in Honor of Francis Peabody Magoun, Jr*. New York: New York University Press, 92–119.

Sofaer, J. R. 2006. *The Body as Material Culture: A Theoretical Osteoarchaeology*. Cambridge, Cambridge University Press.

Sommer, R. S., F. E. Zachos, M. Street, O. Jöris, A. Skog & N. Benecke 2008. 'Late Quaternary distribution dynamics and phylogeography of the red deer (*Cervus elaphus*) in Europe', *Quaternary Science Reviews* **27**(7–8): 714–733.

Sorrell, P. 1996. 'Alcuin's "comb" riddle', *Neophilologus* **80**: 311–318.

Soulat, J. 2011. 'Redécouverte d'un peigne ajourée en alliage cuivreux dans les réserves du Musée d'Archéologie nationale (fin VIIe-début VIIIe siècle)', *Antiquités Nationales* **41**: 119–125.

Steane, J. 2001. *The Archaeology of Power*. Stroud, Tempus.

Stenton, F. 1943. *Anglo-Saxon England, 3rd Edition*. Oxford, Oxford University Press.

Stickney, B. 2011. 'How to Find Moose Antler Sheds: A Registered Maine Guide shares her stories about looking for moose antlers, a growing outdoor hobby'. [Accessed May 2011. Available from: http://www.suite101.com/content/how-to-find-moose-antler-sheds-a373774#ixzz1W3k1etvP].

Storli, I. 1993. 'Sami Viking Age pastoralism – or "The Fur Trade Paradigm" reconsidered', *Norwegian Archaeological Review* **26**(1): 1–20.

Storli, I. 1996. 'On the historiography of Sami reindeer pastoralism', *Acta Borealia* **1**: 81–115.

Sutcliffe, A. J. 1973a. 'Further notes on bones and antlers chewed by deer and other ungulates', *Deer* **4**: 73–82.

Sutcliffe, A. J. 1973b. 'Similarity of Bones and Antlers Gnawed by Deer to Human Artefacts', *Nature* **246**: 428–430.

Sutcliffe, A. J. 1974. 'Similarity of bones and antlers gnawed by deer to human artefacts', *Deer* **3**: 270–272.

Svanberg, F. 2003. *Decolonizing the Viking Age 1: Acta Archaeologica Lundensia Series 8 No. 43*. Stockholm, Almqvist & Wiksell.

Sykes, N. J. 2005. 'Hunting for the Anglo-Normans: Zooarchaeological Evidence for Medieval Identity', in A. Pluskowski (ed.), *Just Skin and Bones? New Perspectives on Human–Animal Relations in the Historical Past. British Archaeological Reports, International Series 1410*. Oxford: Archaeopress, 73–80.

Sykes, N. J. 2007. *The Norman Conquest: a Zooarchaeological Perspective. British Archaeological Reports International Series 1656.* Oxford, Archaeopress.

Sykes, N. J. 2010. 'Deer, land, knives and halls: social change in early medieval England', *Antiquaries Journal* 90: 175–193.

Taylor, T. F. 2010. *The Artificial Ape.* New York, Palgrave MacMillan.

Terry, P. 1965. *The Song of Roland.* Indianapolis, Bobs-Merrill Company.

Tesch, S. 1987. *Kyrkolunden: en historisk och arkeologisk tillbakablick.* Märsta, Sweden: Sigtunahem.

Thorsteinsson, A. 1968. 'The Viking Burial Place at Pierowall, Westray, Orkney', in Niclasen, B. (ed.), *The Fifth Viking Congress: Tórshavn, July 1965.* Tórshavn, Føroya Landsstyri.

Took, R. 2004. *Running with Reindeer: Encounters in Russian Lapland.* London, John Murray.

Tschan, F. J. 2002. Adam of Bremen, 'History of the Archbishops of Hamburg-Bremen'. New York, Columbia University Press.

Ulbricht, I. 1978. *Die Geweihverarbeitung in Haithabu. Die Ausgrabungen in Haithabu 7,* Neumünster: Wachholtz.

Ulbricht, I. 1980. 'Middelalderlig kamproduktion i Slesvig', *Hikuin 6.*

Ulriksen, J. 1998. *Anløbspladser. besejling og bebyggelse i Danmark mellem 200 og 1100 e.Kr.* Roskilde, Vikingeskibshallen.

Ulriksen, J. 2004. 'Danish Coastal Landing Places and their Relation to Navigation and Trade', in J. Hines, A. Lane & M. Redknap (eds), *Land, Sea and Home: Settlement in the Viking Period. SMA Monograph 20.* Leeds, Society for Medieval Archaeology.

van der Leeuw, S. 1993. 'Giving the Potter a Choice. Conceptual aspects of pottery techniques', in P. Lemonnier (ed.), *Technological Choices: Transformation in Material Cultures since the Neolithic.* London: Routledge, 233–288.

Vaughan, R. 1958. 'The chronicle attributed to John of Wallingford', in *Camden Miscellany* 21: p. i–xv, 1–74, London: Royal Historical Society.

Venclová, N. 2002. 'The Venerable Bede, druidic tonsure and archaeology', *Antiquity* 76: 458–471.

Vretemark, M. 1989. 'Kammakeriavfallet – en osteologisk analys', in K. Carlsson (ed.), *Arkeologi i Kungahalla 1989.* Länsstyrelsen i Göteborg och Bohuslän, 57–66.

Vretemark, M. 1997. 'Raw materials and urban comb manufacturing in medieval Scandinavia', *Anthropozoologica* **25–26**: 201–206.

Wallace, J. 1693. *A Description of the Isles of Orkney.*

Wallace-Hadrill, J. M. 1982. *The Long-haired Kings.* London, Methuen.

Wattenbach, W. & E. Diimmler 1873. *Monumenta Alcuiniaua (Bibliotheca Rermn Germanicarum 6)*. Berlin.

Walleström, T. 2000. 'The Saami between east and west in the Middle Ages: An archaeological contribution to the history of reindeer breeding', *Acta Borealia* 17(1): 3–39.

Weber, B. 2007. *Vesle Hjerkinn – Kongens Gård Og Sælehus, Norske oldfunn 21*. Oslo, Universitetets kulturhistoriske museer.

Welander, R. D. E., C. E. Batey & T. G. Cowie 1987. 'A Viking burial fom Kneep, Uig, Isle of Lewis', *Proceedings of the Society of Antiquaries of Scotland* 117: 147–174.

White, R. 2006. 'The women of Brassempouy: a century of research and interpretation', Journal *of Archaeological Method and Theory* 13 (4): 251–304.

Whitelock, D. 1979. *English Historical Documents* c. *500–1042*. London, Eyre Methuen.

Whiten, A., J. Goodall, W. C. Mcgrew, T. Nishida, V. Reynolds, Y. Sugiyama, C. E. G. Tutin, R. W. Wrangham & C. Boesch 1999. 'Cultures In Chimpanzees', *Nature* 399: 682–685.

Williams, H. 2003. 'Material culture as memory: combs and cremation in early medieval Britain', *Early Medieval Europe* 12(2): 89–128.

Williams, H. 2004. 'Artefacts in Early Medieval graves: A new perspective', in R. Collins & J. Gerrard (eds), *Debating Late Antiquity in Britain AD300–700. British Archaeological Reports British Series 365*. Oxford: Archaeopress, 89–102.

Williams, H. 2006. *Death and Memory in Early Medieval Britain*. Cambridge, Cambridge University Press.

Williams, H. 2007. 'Transforming Body and Soul: Toilet Implements in Early Anglo-Saxon Graves', in S. Semple (ed.), *Early Medieval Mortuary Practices: Anglo-Saxon Studies in Archaeology and History 14*. Oxbow and Oxford University School of Archaeology: Oxford, 66–91.

Wilson, A. S., M. P. Richards, B. Stern, R. C. Janaway, A. M. Pollard & D. J. Tobin 2007. 'Information on Grauballe man from his hair', in P. Asingh & N. Lynnerup (eds), *Grauballe Man: An Iron Age Bog Body Revisited*. Moesgaard: Jutland Archaeological Society, 188–195.

Wilson, A. S., T. Taylor, M. C. Ceruti, J. A. Chavez, J. Reinhard, V. Grimes, W. Meier-Augenstein, L. Cartmell, B. Stern, M. P. Richards, M. Worobey, I. Barnes & T. P. Gilbert 2007. 'Stable isotope and DNA evidence for ritual sequences in Inca child sacrifice', *Proceedings of the National Academy of Sciences of the United States of America* 104(42): 16456–16461.

Wilson, D. 1992. *Anglo-Saxon Paganism*. London, Routledge.

Winstead, K. A. 2003. 'St Katherine's Hair', in J. Jenkins & K. J. Lewis (eds), *St Katherine of Alexandria*. Turnhout: Brepols, 170–199.

Wylie, A. 1985. 'The reaction against analogy', *Advances in Archaeological Method and Theory* 8(3): 63–111.

Zachrisson, I. 2008. 'The Sämi and their Interaction with the Nordic People', in S. Brink & N. S. Price (eds), *The Viking World*. London: Routledge, 32–39.

Zahavi, A. & A. Zahavi 1997. *The Handicap Principle: A Missing Piece of Darwin's Puzzle*. New York, Oxford University Press.

Zurowski, K. 1974. 'Zmiekczanie porozy i kości stosowane przez wytwórców w starozytnosci i we wczesnym średniowieczu', *Acta Universitatis Nicolai Copernici, Archaeologia (Torun)* 4: 3–23.

List of Illustrations

Chapter-Facing Pages

Figures

7. Combmaking debris from Hungate, York. (Image courtesy York Archaeological Trust)
8. Contemporary hairstyling: what associations do these different styles have for you? (Drawing by Steve Ashby)
9. The toolkit of contemporary haircare ritual. (Image by Alison Leonard)
10. The 'Venus of Brassempouy'. (Drawing by Hayley Saul)
11. An Iron-Age mirror from Desborough, Northamptonshire. (Drawing by Nick Griffiths)
12. An Iron-Age comb from Tanworth-in-Arden, Warks. (Drawing by Candy Stevens)
13. The Niederdollendorf Stone, Germany. Note sword (passive) and comb (active). (Drawing by Hayley Saul)
14. Haircuts of contention: the (a) Roman and (b) Celtic tonsures. (Drawing by Steve Ashby)
15. Peacock and deer. (Images by '10mpx cg' and Ruth Carden)
16. A Pre-Viking miniature 'beard' comb. (Drawing Hayley Saul, courtesy Trustees of National Museums Scotland)
17. St Cuthbert's comb. (Drawing by Nick Griffiths)
18. Hair behaviour in sculpture, Clonmacnoise, Ireland. (Image by David Petts)
19. Hair and status in sculpture: the Brough of Birsay, Orkney. (Drawing by Steve Ashby)
20. A so-called 'horse comb' from Viking-Age Sweden. (Drawing by Hayley Saul)
21. A well-made comb and case from a grave at Skaill Bay, Orkney. (Image by Steve Ashby, courtesy Trustees of the National Museums of Scotland)
22. A double-sided comb typical of Anglo-Saxon England and 'Pictish' northern Scotland. (Drawing by Pat Walsh, Northamptonshire Archaeology)
23. An ornate 'hogbacked' comb from York, dating to the pre-Viking period. (Image by Steve Ashby, courtesy York Museums Trust)
24. An ornate pre-Viking comb from Orkney, northern Scotland. (Drawing by Hayley Saul, courtesy Orkney Museum)
25. An ornate handled comb from York. (Drawing by Nick Griffiths)
26. A large, early Viking comb from Birka, Sweden. (Drawing by Pat Walsh, Northamptonshire Archaeology)
27. A late Viking-Age comb from Denmark. (Drawing by Pat Walsh, Northamptonshire Archaeology)
28. An irregular, late Viking-Age comb from York. (Drawing by Hayley Saul)

Index

Also available from Amberley Publishing

The
Kings & Queens
of
Anglo-Saxon
England

TIMOTHY VENNING

Available from all good bookshops or to order direct
Please call **01453–847–800**
www.amberleybooks.com

Also available from Amberley Publishing

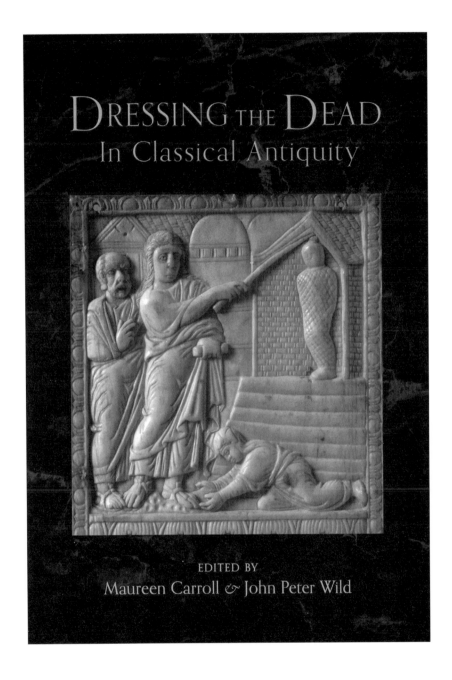

DRESSING THE DEAD
In Classical Antiquity

EDITED BY
Maureen Carroll & John Peter Wild

Also available from Amberley Publishing

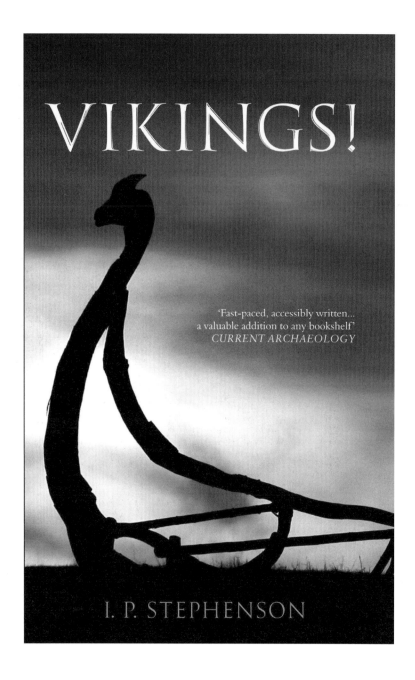

Available from all good bookshops or to order direct
Please call **01453–847–800**
www.amberleybooks.com

Also available from Amberley Publishing

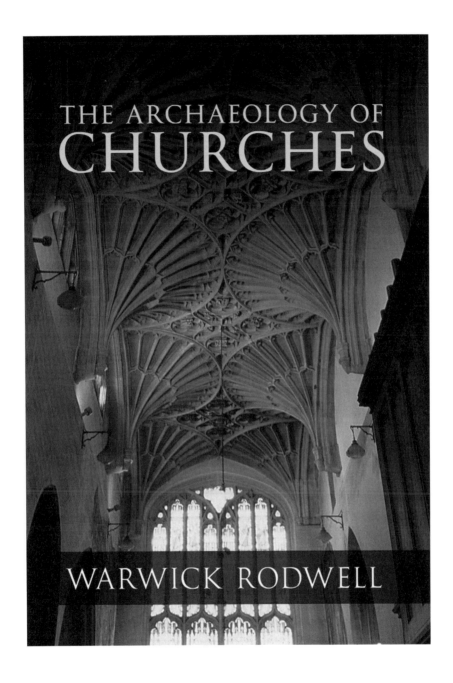

Also available from Amberley Publishing

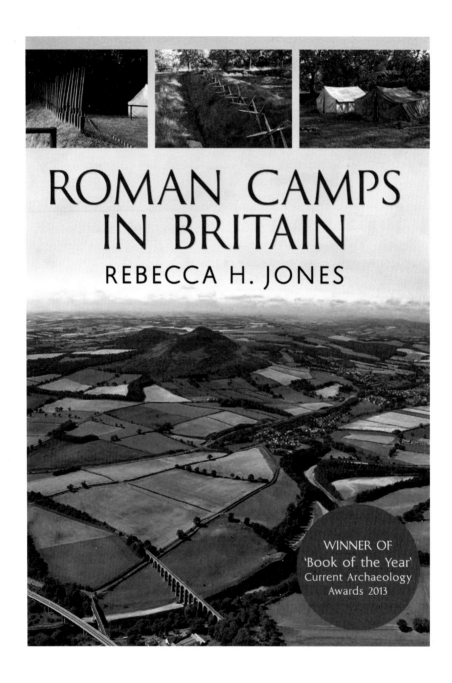

ROMAN CAMPS
IN BRITAIN

REBECCA H. JONES

WINNER OF
'Book of the Year'
Current Archaeology
Awards 2013

Available from all good bookshops or to order direct
Please call **01453-847-800**
www.amberleybooks.com